The Last Days of Hythe Harbour

by
MAURICE YOUNG

**Published by the Hythe Civic Society ~ AD 2000
with support from
Millennium "Awards for All" and
Shepway District Council**

© Text by Maurice Young
© Maps and illustrations by Janine Umbers

ISBN 1 900101 20 3

Acknowledgements

This Book was made possible by Grants to the Hythe
Civic Society under the Millennium Festival Awards for All Programme,
and from Shepway District Council Arts Culture and Leisure Fund.

The Author and Artist are grateful to Richard Scarth for help with word processing and photography,
to the Librarians, Archivists and other staff at Hythe, Folkestone, Whitfield, Canterbury and Maidstone,
to Mr Crunden, Dr P. Cuming, Mr and Mrs Griggs, Mrs Marston, Mr Mealham,
Mr Osborne, The Rev'd Marcus Ramshaw, Miss Sharp
and various members of Hythe Civic Society and its Committee.
Other Acknowledgements are in the text.

Text : Maurice Young
Maps and Illustrations : Janine Umbers

Prologue

This booklet attempts to outline the final years of the one-time harbour or haven at Hythe in Kent. The problem has been to interpret the information in the old records, which are never explicit. Terms such as 'old port', 'new port' and 'old stade' may refer to different locations at different times and are difficult to place with certainty.

That there was once a harbour, and a thriving one, with war-ships, merchant-men and fishing vessels sheltering from the open sea, is not in doubt. Its general location is known but it moved over time as did the access channels and openings into it. It certainly began near West Hythe, 3 miles to the west of the present town. There was a Bronze-age settlement here, fisherfolk one deduces, and near here later was the Roman Portus Lemanis, below Lympne, at the very start of Stone Street, the main road to Canterbury. Romney Bay then received the waters (and silt and debris too) of three rivers, the Tillingham, Brede, and Rother (formerly the Limen), and of other lesser streams, pouring down from the uplands behind. A bank of shingle protected the inner coastline from the open sea, and within that a desolate area of shingle banks, sand and mud flats, with inlets and creeks, and a sheltered lagoon with access possibly from the west near Greatstone and also from the east where one of the estuaries of the Rother met the incoming sea near present-day Seabrook. There may have been other inlets too, south from the Port.

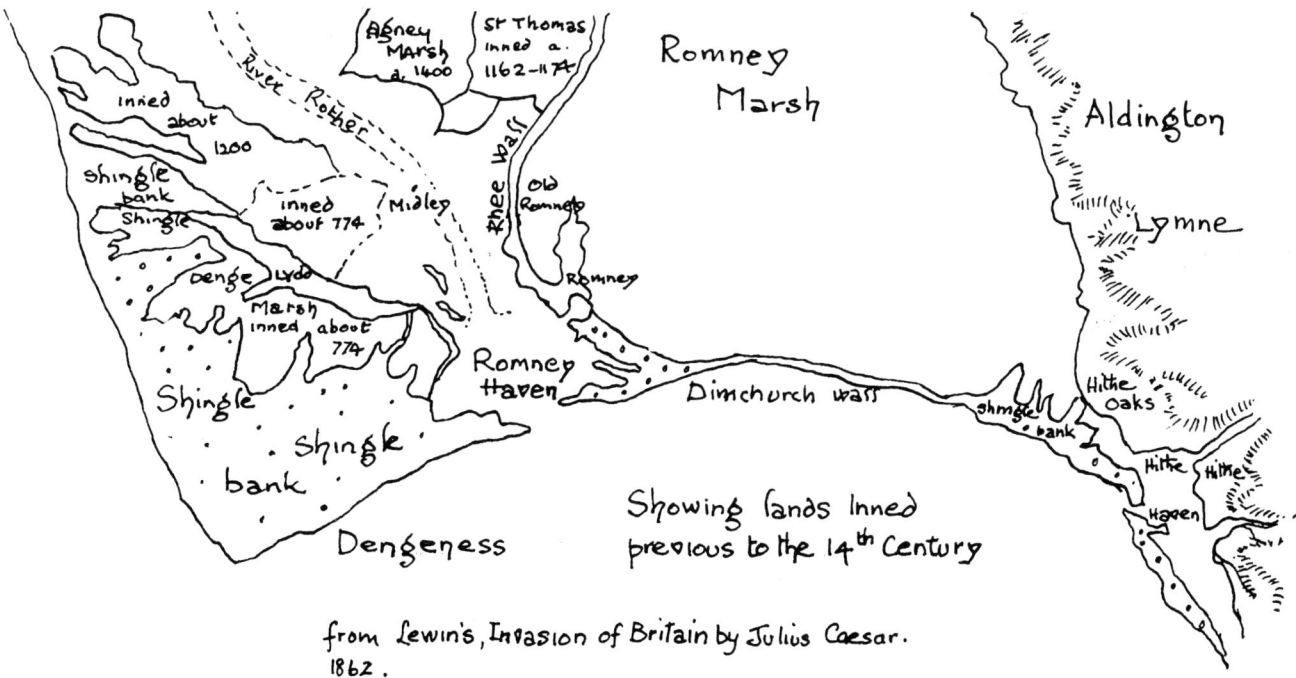

from Lewin's, Invasion of Britain by Julius Caesar. 1862.

At safe anchor here in this calm water rode the tiny fishing boats, and the larger merchant-men which supported the occupying Roman army - bringing reinforcements, warmer clothing and other supplies for troops on look-out in the far north, and mail from home. Most visible would have been the ships of Classis Brittanica, the war fleet, protecting this vulnerable coast so close to the continental mainland from raiders and pirates. Later a large stone fort, 10 acres in area, was built above the landing point - the ruins at Stutfall (occupied probably 275-350AD) can be seen still. But in the dark unrecorded period after the Romans' departure in the early 5th Century, there came land-slip, dramatic changes to the coast-line with higher sea-levels, and a build-up of

silt, the lagoon becoming smaller and the approach channels narrower and shallower, even as sea-going ships were getting larger, until ships could no longer reach the old quayside and even the fishermen were forced to unload their tiny boats further and further east; their habitations naturally were moved with them.

The natural process of silting up was the problem the citizens of the tiny town had to contend with if they were to continue to take advantage of their location as a mercantile and defensive port.

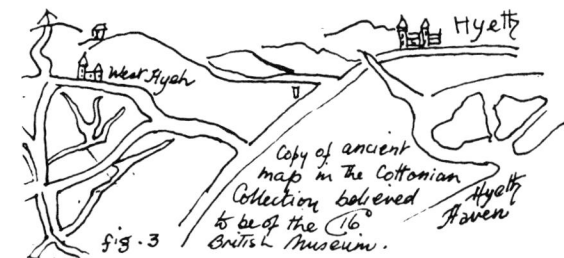

Initially the migration eastwards was successful: the town grew and prospered through farming, fishing and continental trade; the straggling line of houses stabilised on the present site of Hythe so that by 1080 the citizens were in no doubt where to build their new Norman-style church - on the hillside scarcely 100 yards above the water's edge, at the very centre of their town as of their lives. That first building remains at the core of the present St Leonard's Church. Even before the Norman Invasion Hythe was already important enough to be one - the central one - of the five towns bound together in that confederation The Cinque Ports, set up to provide coastal defence at the King's need, and of growing importance when safe cross-channel passage became vital to the Anglo-Norman realm. But access to the sea was becoming more and more difficult: approach from the west had long been impossible, and there were two dramatic alterations to the course of the Rother during violent hurricanes in the period 1250 - 1287 with the destruction by high roaring tides of the outer protective bank.

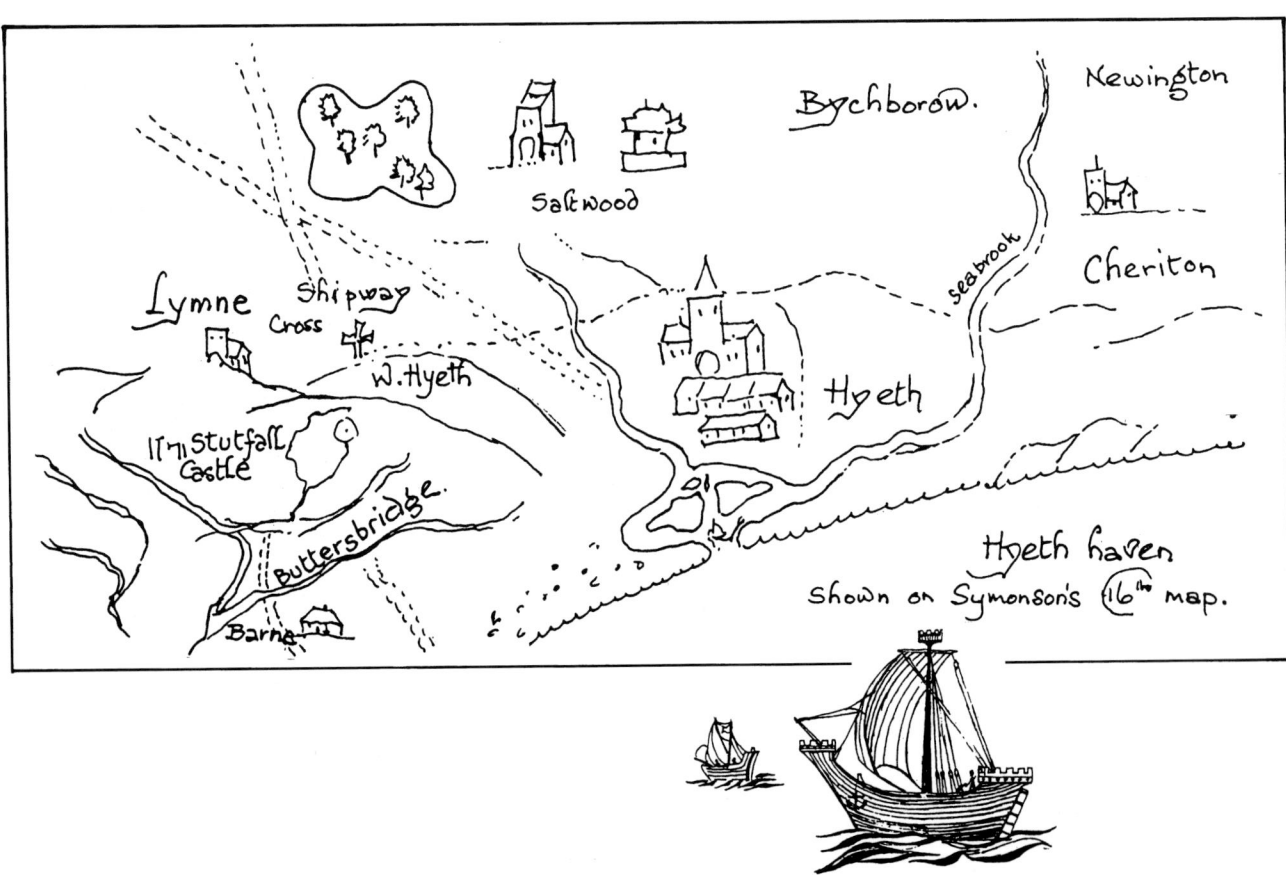

The documentary record of the battle to keep the harbour open against the forces of nature is tantalisingly vague. Maurice Young has sought out the references, and quotes from or summarises the frantic efforts, such as the decision taken in 1654 to construct a sluice to scour the silt away by releasing a head of water from the high ground. It was all in vain. By 1679 the harbour was abandoned - there is not even a sign of it on the 'Hospital Map' of 1684.

The Maps and Illustrations are by Janine Umbers based partly on the written text and partly on other sources, especially the geological record. The intention is to relate the documents to the layout of the town we know today, but she admits to being speculative and even controversial in the details.

SMR no. TR13 SE50 KE8905
67-69 High Street.
See Dia. IV p.51.

White Hart

Wealden Hall House
The builder is known from his mark on the King Post. He died in 1360.

In the S.E. the beams are naturally bleached not darkened. These steps rise up to the level of Dentall Street

Mounting Block.

There were Early buildings here also. Maybe stables

This is the North side where the original entrance was once facing the main street.

There is a record in 1413 of 4d paid for a days work by 'Slow bregge' and mending stair before the door of the Common Hall. This building could have been the hall referred to. If so the Accounts which provide us with so much information were written here or in the previous building which was burnt down.

This is a 14th Century Whealden Hall House still extant in Hythe.

Contents

		Page
Chapter I	The Place and the Problem	9
Chapter II	The New Haven	13
Chapter III	The Hoye	23
Chapter IV	Cutting Out	30
Chapter V	The Sluice	34
Chapter VI	Swan Song	41
Chapter VII	Last Days	49

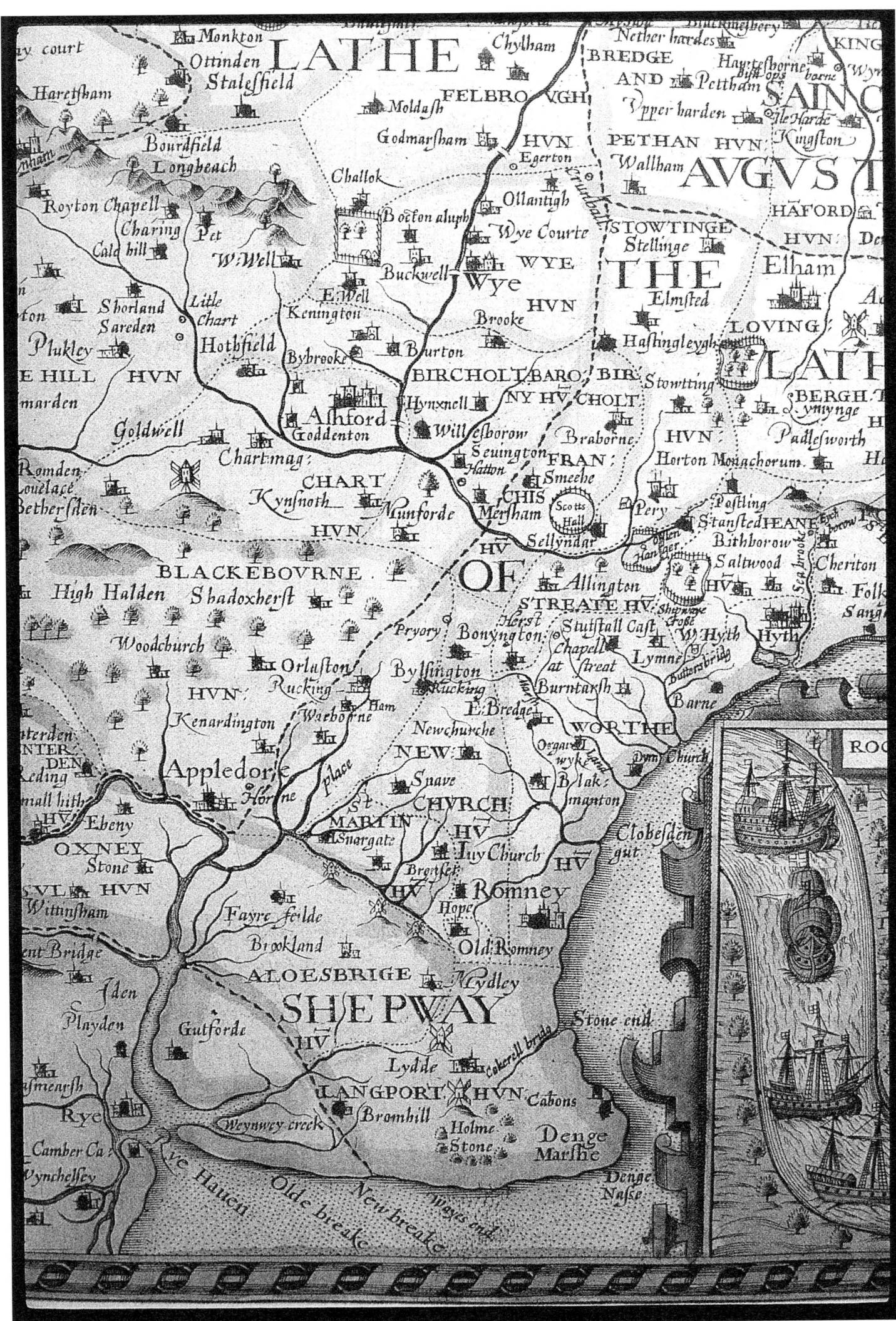

Chapter I
The Place and the Problem

The coast of South East England bordering the Channel is a place of pebble beaches and forgotten harbours. The constant easterly drift of shingle through the action of wind and sea over many centuries has caused an ever changing coastline. One result is the great headland of Dungeness, jutting out into the sea from the Kent coast. The fortunes of the five ancient Cinque Ports of Hastings, Romney, Hythe, Dover and Sandwich, and of the two Ancient Towns of Rye and Winchelsea, were also closely bound up with the changing nature of this coastline. Winchelsea, relocated after its destruction in great storms, is now far from the sea, and the narrow river entrance leading to the harbour at Rye needs constant protection from drifting shingle. As for the Cinque Ports, formerly supplying many ships for the service of the King, Dover survives, but even there, significant development was not possible until the late 19th century, when the Admiralty Pier was extended far enough into deep water to arrest the silting action of the sea. Sandwich, once an important harbour, was silted up by the 15th century, and has declined to a riverside quay for small vessels. At Hastings, the harbour was blocked by the 12th century, and in the ensuing years, it has been necessary to launch and recover boats over a beach formed by the accumulation of shingle.

Dover Harbour

The harbours of the two remaining members of the original Cinque Ports suffered the worst fate. As a result of the build up of shingle over a long period, the towns of Romney and Hythe are now distant from the sea, and although a few fishing boats still work from open beaches at Hythe, there are no visible remains at either place to show the existence of harbours. They have completely vanished.

Looking at Hythe in particular, by great good fortune, many ancient documents have survived in the extensive town archives, including the records of the Corporation and Council of Hythe over a lengthy period. Quotations from the documents occur throughout this account, and although the language poses certain problems, these fascinating sources allow us a glimpse of the story of the old harbour of Hythe.

Any person who reads the Corporation documents will not fail to be impressed by their essential formality, if 'impressed' be quite the right word. 'Frustrated' would be more appropriate. Formality and repetition are frequent, and most documents contain archaic forms of expression. A brief explanation of some of these old forms of notation will serve as a prelude to the main story. The double 'ff' was used for 'F', the letter 'y' was frequently found in place of 'i', the letter 'e' was often added to the end of a word, and capital letters were used to begin a word where they would not now be used in English. A form of abbreviation known as an 'elison' consisted of two words run together, for example 'shalbe' or 'shalbee' for 'shall be', and 'thone' for 'the one' and 'thother' for 'the other'. The use of an archaic letter called the 'thorn' occurs in all the source documents used for this story. The 'thorn' was an old way of writing 'th' and had the appearance of a letter 'y'. Hence the word 'the' looked like 'ye'. In this account, the word has been transcribed as 'the.'

There is no consistency in spelling in these old documents, and for example 'capston' or 'capstayn' are used for capstan, and 'bote', 'boate' or 'bot' for boat. Various spellings of the name Hythe occur, including 'Hethe,' 'Hith', 'Hithe,' 'Heath' and even 'Hyde'. 'Forreynors' were not people from a foreign country, but those from outside the parish or Liberty of Hythe. Obsolete words occur, for example 'rypper' or 'rippier', meaning a fish trader who came with pack horses to buy fish at the shore. This word is thought to be derived either from the Latin word 'ripa' or from 'rip', a pannier basket set across a horse's back for the carrying of fish. Some words had a slightly different meaning. 'Farm', often spelled 'ffarme' or 'ferme' did not, in the legal context have the familiar agricultural meaning, but implied a tenancy in return for the payment of an annual rent. 'Fee farm' was such a tenancy which could be inherited.

Double year dating is a feature of documentary sources used in this account. Until 1752 the year for legal and administrative purposes ran from March 25th to March 24th. There were also regnal years and ordinary calendar years. In a legal context, a day prior to March 25th in the calendar year 1413 was in the previous legal year of 1412, hence the expression 1412/13.

In case the reader imagines that there is somewhere in the Town Archive a description of an old world haven or harbour, filled with picturesque boats and colourful seamen, it is worth making the point that there is no detailed record of life in Hythe during past centuries in the records of the Corporation, known as the Minutes of Assembly. Alas, no such canvas exists, except as an exercise of the imagination. The reality is that the task of describing the last days of Hythe harbour involves the patient extraction of as much sense as possible from documents whose background was doubtless well known to those people who were alive at the time, but who are now long dead.

There are frequent references in the Minutes of the Assemblies of the Corporation of Hythe to 'The Town and Cinque Port of Hythe.' Hythe was granted a Charter in the reign of Queen Elizabeth I, and by that Charter in the year 1575, the town was incorporated in the Major, Jurats, and Commonalty. Before 1575 the town was governed by a Bailiff and Jurats.

This 1575 charter provided that an Assembly should be held each year to elect a Mayor, and that the meeting should take place on 2nd February, the day of the Feast of the Purification of the Blessed Virgin Mary, often called Candlemas.

The Jurats were the senior men of the Corporation, and from their number the Mayor was chosen. The Jurats were in their turn, chosen from among the Common Councilmen of the Corporation, who were elected from the Freemen of the Corporation.

The Common Councilmen were collectively called the Commonalty, and the phrase 'Mayor, Jurats and Commonalty' occurs many times in the source documents used for this history, especially in legal papers relating to the letting and leasing of lands.

The geographic area governed by the Corporation constituted the 'Liberty of the Town and Port of Hythe.' The Liberty consisted of the parish of St. Leonard Hythe, together with part of the parish of West Hythe and part of the parish of Aldington, the last named being separated from the main part of Aldington parish. The Liberty did not include land eastward of Twiss Road. That road was named after an army officer involved in the construction of defences in the Napoleonic war period, and it is one of several ways to the sea from the town. A memory of the harbour is preserved in the name of another of these routes - Stade Street. These streets, running in a southerly direction from the old town to the sea, pass through newer areas of the town which have developed on top of an expanse of shingle, deposited over a long period which saw the decline of the harbour. *(End Map)*

The Borough of Hythe was extended eastward from Twiss Road as far as Battery Point in Victorian times. The new land included Seabrook and the area occupied at the time of writing by the buildings and golf course of the Hythe Imperial. These areas were not within the control of the Corporation of Hythe in earlier times, a matter of some significance when we come to study the possible location of the harbour of Hythe.

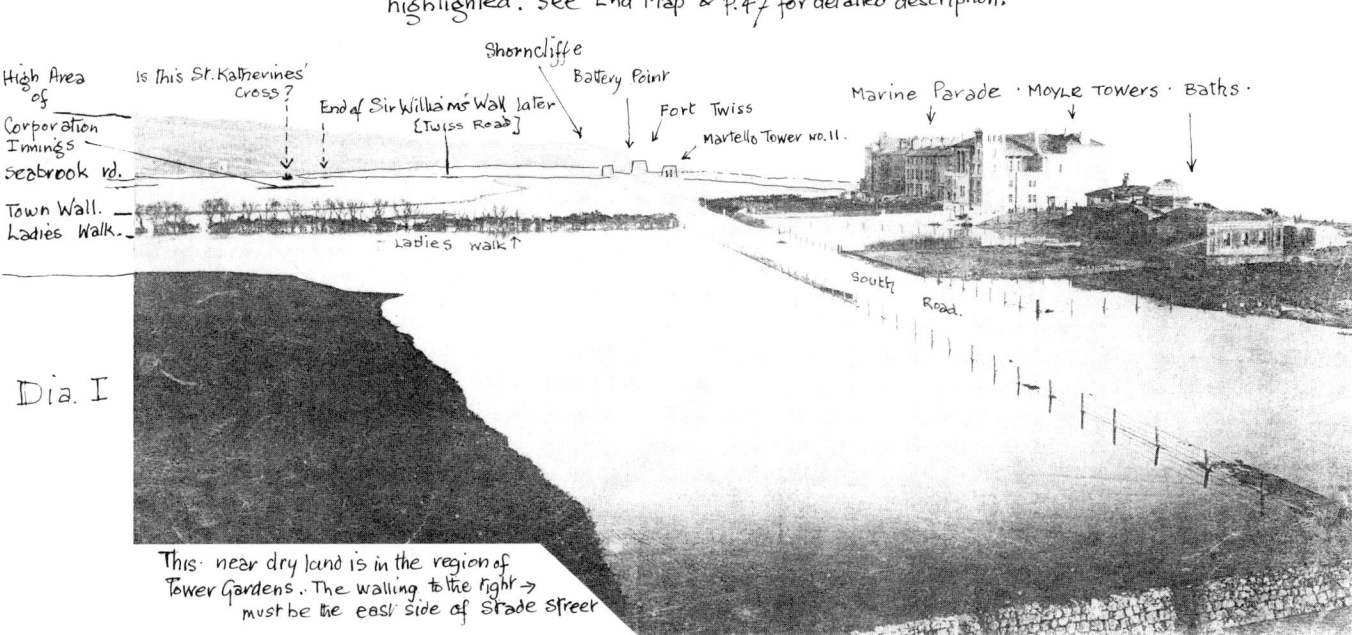

The Municipal Corporations Act of 1835 introduced radical changes, when the Mayor, Jurats and Commonalty were replaced by a Council consisting of a Mayor, Aldermen and Burgesses. From that time onward we speak of a Council, though as the writer well remembers from his childhood, the Town often prided itself on being a 'Corporation', and Hythe retains its title as one of the original Cinque Ports.

A 19th century dispute involving Hythe Town Council has a direct bearing on the history of the harbour. In 1871 the Board of Trade gave notice to the Council to discontinue construction of a large groyne known as the Twiss Fort Groyne. A groyne usually consists of a line of timber piles and planking, running down a beach at right angles to the shore with the object of arresting beach movement. In addition to the problem of the groyne, in the same year 1871, the Chief Coastguard Officer at Hythe wrote to a local resident, giving him notice to stop taking shingle, sand etc. from the beach at Hythe below the high water mark. The resident passed the letter on to the Borough Surveyor. On receipt of this letter, the Town Clerk Mr George Wilks sent a reply to the Chief Coastguard Officer on 25th October 1871, stating that Hythe Town Council claimed the foreshore between low and high water mark, and that the Board of Trade had no right to interfere in the matter. The Chief Coastguard Officer forwarded the Town Clerk's letter to the Board of Trade. As a result, the Board of Trade wrote to Mr Wilks, asking him to supply information under which the Council claimed title to the foreshore which was vested in the Crown.

The Parvise.
The priest's room above St. Leonard's south porch became the Town Council meeting place for about 250 years until 1794 when it moved to the New Town Hall in place of the 1660 Market Hall & Court Hall.

Following the advice and encouragement of Mr Wilks, members of the Town Council decided to defend their believed ownership of the foreshore at Hythe and thus to dispute the opinion of the Board of Trade that, according to a presumption of the law, title to the foreshore at Hythe would be vested in the Crown. In other words, the burden of proof lay with the Council to prove that they, and not the Crown, were owners of the foreshore.

The Council authorized Mr Wilks to have the Town's records searched and interpreted, and in a subsequent report to his Council, Mr Wilks declared that 'the whole of the Charters, books and documents in the old Town Hall were thoroughly gone through and searches were made at the Record Office, the British Museum, the Lambeth Library and at Romney and other Ports, the assistance of a specialist Mr R.E.G.Kirk, being obtained to assist in the search and in the translation of the old Charters and documents.' The 'old Town Hall' would, presumably, have been a reference to the Parvise, a room over the south porch of the parish church, long associated with the secular Corporation of Hythe.

The sizeable task of searching the Town's records occupied the persons involved for six years, and was not completed until 1877. The statement finally submitted on behalf of the Council was, however, rejected by the Crown. In 1886 the Solicitor of Woods and Forests, who acted for the Crown, filed an 'Information against the Mayor, Aldermen and Burgesses of Hythe.' After a further period, the dispute was finally settled by a compromise, which resulted in the Town Council retaining rights to the foreshore between the old borough boundary near Fort Twiss, and Fort Sutherland, which was situated slightly to the westward of Fisherman's Beach. This section of the foreshore would be covered by a present day visitor starting at the seaward end of Twiss Road, and walking west to the point where the sea wall ends at Fisherman's Beach. The Crown claimed the foreshore westward of that point as far as the Grand Redoubt, which can be seen by looking westwards from Fisherman's Beach towards the Grand Redoubt which still exists. The Government had already purchased this stretch, known as Beachy Outlands, from the Town Council for use as a musketry range, and the area is now familiar in sight and sound to residents of Hythe as Hythe Ranges. *(End Map)*

The prime purpose of the search of the Town's records was to support the Council in their belief that they and their forebears had for centuries past been owners of the foreshore, especially below the high water level. But, as a by-product of that search, the former Town Clerk was able to prepare a series of twenty eight articles, printed by the Hythe and Sandgate Advertiser in 1884 and 1885, and one of those articles in particular has proved of considerable value in preparing this account of the long vanished harbour of Hythe.

Chapter II
The New Haven

The eastward drift of shingle, which had such a disastrous effect upon the Cinque Ports, was also a factor in the silting up of two lost harbours near the present town of Hythe, at Limene and West Hythe. It is clear from documentary evidence that by the 15th century, Hythe harbour was also in trouble, and by Henry VIII's reign (1509 - 1547), it was reduced to a narrow channel which, though Leland called it a 'pretty road', was subject to old and familiar problems. The story of attempts to keep the harbour open over a period from the 15th to the 17th centuries can be pieced together from the Minutes of Assembly of the Corporation of Hythe and a variety of counterpart copies of leases of Corporation lands and properties.

Evidence of work on the harbour in the 15th century is to be found in the Books of Jurates Accounts for the years 1412 - 1413. Fortunately, these old documents were transcribed and translated by the late Revd. T.S. Frampton, and his neatly written record is now in the Hythe Town Archive.

> 'Item, paid to John Lucas, in part payment for digging 19 rods in the New Port, price per rod, 3s. 4d. and for digging 106 rods from the 'Havene' to the 'Eastbregge', price per rod, 20d. And for 380 rods from the 'Ermytage' to 'Westh Hethe', price per rod 12d. as appears [by] the particulars of payment ("Item solut' Johni Lucas in ptem soluc' p fodiac' de xix virg' nouo portu cap' p virga iijs. iiijd. & p fodiac' de Cvj virg' a le hauene vsqz le Eastbregge cap' p virg' xx d. & p CCC iiij^{xx} virg' a le Ermytage vsqz Westh Hethe cap' p virga xijd. vt pz p cellas soluc'") — £30. 10s.'
>
> 'Item, paid to Thomas Shyngelere, in part payment of 33s. 4d. for making a new bridge by 'Westhethe' — 20s.'
>
> 'Sum — (sic)
>
> 26d. 'Elsewhere'
> Item, paid for expenses, and the returns of two writs,

The previous quotation contains references to money in pre-decimal currency which may not be familiar to all readers. The pound was formerly divided into 20 shillings, each of 12 'old' pennies. Amounts were expressed in pounds, shillings, and pence, (£.s.d.) using symbols derived from the Latin 'libra' for the pound (£), the Greek letter 'sigma' for shillings (s), and the Latin 'denarius' (d) for pence. Smaller amounts occur in the form of the halfpenny and farthing, being respectively 1/2 and 1/4 of a penny.

Two other payments were made for breaking a dam at an unknown location described as the 'Hermitage', the second in order that water might flow into the delvez or diggings.

113

'Item, paid to John Daly and William Wodour, for 9 rods, at 2s. per rod; in all	18s.'	
'Item, paid to the same John Daly, for other 9 rods, at 2s. per rod; in all	18s.'	
'Item, paid to the same John Daly, on the *Vigil of the Purification of the Blessed Mary	2s.	2d.'
'Item, the same reckon paid to William Mawere, on Saturday* next after the Feast of [our] Lord's Ascension, as appears by the payments of this year, for digging in "lez Delvez"	20s.'	
'Item, paid to the same William, for digging 20 rods, at 18d. per rod	30s.'	
'Item, paid to the same William, for digging 10 rods and a half, at 18d. per rod	15s.	9d.'
'Item, paid to Stephen Mersch, on *Thursday, next after the Feast of the Translation of St. Thomas the Martyr, for digging between the two bridges	6s.	8d.'
'Item, paid to the same Stephen Mersch, for digging in the same ditch, *on Sunday next after the Feast of the Translation of St. Thomas the Martyr	6s.	8d.'
'Item, paid to the same Stephen Mersch, on *Sunday, next before the Feast of St. Margaret, for digging in the same ditch	11s.	1d.'
'Item, paid paid (sic) to the same Stephen, on *Sunday, next before the Feast of St. James, for digging in the same ditch	5s.'	
'Item, paid to the same Stephen by receipt of divers labourers working with him; viz to one by name Thomelyn, for two days work and a half, and John Brakbourne and others, as appears by the payment of their days' work ("Itm solut' eidm Stepho p recept' diuso3 laborario3 secu laboranc' vidlt vni noie suo Thomelyn p ij jnet9 + de + Joh Brakbone + alijs vt p3 p soluc' jurnetaz sua3")	19s.	10d.'

'Costs of Digging.'

> 'Item, paid to Henry Chacherell, for our portion on
> the confirmation of the King's Charter —— 104s. 5½d.'
>
> 'Sum — £17. 8s. 11½d.'

84.
> 'Imprimis, on Monday, viz. 6th March, when the Port was
> opened; in bread with Nicholas Martyn and John Cook,
> as appears in the allowance of their accounts —— 14d.'
>
> 'Item, the same day, in ale, viz. 15 gallons, with William
> Walton, as appears in the allowance of [his] account —— 22½d.'
>
> 'Item, the same day, in 18 gallons of ale, with John Cowlese,
> as appears in the allowance of his account —— 2s. 3d.'
>
> 'Item, in the following night, for those who worked there,
> in bread with Richard Mongham, as appears by the allow-
> -ance in his account —— 4d.'

Some items included in the Jurates Accounts were for bread and ale supplied to those who worked in what was called the New Port. Bread to the value of 2s.3d., and ale to the value of 9s.3d. were supplied. A number of payments were made for digging in the 'delvez' (i.e. in the diggings) and some payments were for work done by the rod. (A rod = 5 1/2 yards or 5 metres). For example, five sums were paid to Stephen Mersch for work done by himself and others in a ditch between the two bridges. John Lucas was paid £30.10s. for digging 19 rods in the New Port at 3s.4d. per rod, 106 rods from the Haven to the Eastbregge (East bridge) at 20d. per rod, and 380 rods from the Ermytage to West Hythe at 12d. per rod. The payments to John Lucas prompted the Revd. Frampton to observe as follows:-

> The work of excavating in the New Haven would seem to have been either very laborious or very dangerous, the price per rod being 3s. 4d. Between the Haven and the Eastbridge the price was just half that sum. And between the Hermitage and West Hythe only 1s. a rod was charged. If the rod of the 15th Century was as it is now, the distances would be — 104½ yds. in the New Haven; 583 yds. from the Haven to the East bridge; and 2090 yds. from the Hermitage to West Hythe. John Lucas appears to have been paid 10s. short of what he ought to have received.

According to the Revd. Frampton, the new port was opened on March 6th in the year 1413, and the following thoughtful comment appears in his translation, written in purple ink, as ever in his very neat and legible handwriting:-

> * Monday, 6th March, 1413. This day must have been long remembered by the Hythe people, as marking a stage in the return of the tide of prosperity. The labours of the townsfolk were not yet quite ended, for working parties continued to meet for the next ten days, or longer; but this particular day must have been a very joyous one, and it is often referred to as 'the Day when the Port was opened'. According to a calculation made, it appears that the Moon was New the same day — 6th March, 1413. At such times High Water at Hythe is at about 11 a.m. and again somewhat before midnight. This circumstance would account for there being a working, or watching, party in the night following, as is mentioned more than once. Those who composed the party would be told off and stationed at different important points — some of which are specified — to see that all went right as the Tide flowed up. In the absence of moonlight we must imagine the working parties having torches to aid them.

In speaking of the tides, the Revd. Frampton probably had in mind the high Spring tides, for they occur at around mid-day and midnight, and March is one of the months when the Springs are at their highest. But why the night watch? Possibly to check that no overflowing was imminent, always a risk in a low lying area.

In his book 'The Ancient Town of Hythe and St Leonard's Church', the Revd. Dale poses the question 'where was this new harbour?' and went on to suggest that the entrance to the old harbour was just to the east of the entrance to the stade or landing place.

Further developments are set out in a 16th century document concerning a lease of lands to Edward Cressye, a Jurat of Hythe. In the 'thirteenth yere of the raign of our Soveraign ladie Elizabeth', that is, in the year 1570, 'the Barons, portsmen and inhabitants of the Towne and Port of Hethe' granted a twenty one year lease of lands to Edward Cressye, and for the sum of sixteen pounds of lawful money of England, he obtained the use, subject to certain reservations, of 'all and singular the Coen lands, grounds, stones, mersheys, meddowes, pastures, ffedynge playses and fermes' (i.e. the common lands, grounds, stones, marshes, meadows, pastures, feeding places and farms) which had lately been occupied by Thomas Honnywood esquire.

The detailed extent of the land so leased is not stated in the surviving document, but as a conjecture, the amount was a considerable proportion of what was then the Liberty of the Town and Port of Hythe. Among the items reserved by the grantors was pasturage for the space of twenty four hours for the horses, mares and geldings of 'every forreyn Ryppyer coming to the said Towne and Port of Hethe to bye sea ffyshe', and such pasturage was to be 'between St Cleres and the Chapple of the Towne and so to the Stade.'

Dia II. Look first at Front Map.

The Haven within the Liberties; the other called the Stade, without the Liberties. 1566.

1390's
Tax on every sale & purchase. Toll on W. Bridge. Boom & Prosperity

Old Jurats A/c of c1410 shows expenditure for attempted construction of harbour.

[SMR no TR13 SE60-KE 17138]
A hard standing for the beaching of boats. This is a compacted deposit of medium yellowish, greenish brown slightly silty clay with 20% flint pebbles. Also found c14 pottery pieces. It was probably in use from the early C13 to C14 but by the late C14 a rubbish dump sealed the area. Excavated May 1998.

1473 Will. Thomas Honywood mentioned Dentall Garden & a shop as place marker & left money to repair road.

Cannonball, possibly Septaria or mudstone. Widely used in 14° & 15° cen. Found 1998. E of Mill Lane. circum. 9" - 9½". eng. 35/99

St. Katherine. Patron saint of Light houses

(sketch map with annotations including:)
- Centuries on conduit
- Market
- Water supply pipes Dentals field. guns at East Bridge
- Dentall street — 1740 yards between bridges
- 15-15b, 14-98, 16-12-00, 1400
- dam, conjectural line, river flow, less tidal level until 1380. Then rubbish dump creeping South by 1470
- reduced influx so firm ground
- Possible area of 1413 New Port
- 1684 position of river
- St. Johns 1332
- 1555. Knights Innings
- East Bridge
- Newington Meadows, Mill Pond, Mill Lane, cannon & musket ball found
- St. Katherines Croys
- Boundary
- "a pretty rode... a sure got"
- Stade forming Southwards
- 1419 Haven very busy.
- Sun Lane paved for 4 yards.

Was there also a harbour front here? ie Stade, here as mentioned in 1566

1508 Money left to repair road.

1533 Money left for reparation of Haven.

16·12·1549 in Common Hall. People could spread nets, build lodges, capstans & make docks so long as not hurtful to any of the dyke walls or closures.
HT. Archive

Nos 116-120. Hall House 1580-1640

These guns look like basilisks primarily sited to defend waterways in c14 & c15. These were very light guns strapped to heavy base planks or fitted on elementary pivots. Many breech loaders, especially dangerous & inefficient. Henry VIII fortified many important towns.

In 1413. Jurats A/c. Town Archives payments made to Lattiner (ironmonger) for iron for 'Le Gonnys' for Gonnes stonis. Accounts made in Common Hall
9 stones for divers gunnys.
4d paid for days work by 'slow bregge'
4d paid for firing guns when Commonalty made a demonstration
2d paid to Thomas Marchal for bringing the guns from the bridge to the church & for bringing the 'sluttis' (church garments) from the church to E. Bregge

1419 Cinq Port Barons hiring guns for the King

Wool was sold at the Calais Staple. Was the harbour front similar to Calais?

In Calais 1531, gun ports added to fortifications. See also Dover p.

Furthermore, 'every ffysherman of the said Towne and Port of Hethe, and all other ffyshermen that shall presume to come thyther, shall at all tymes during the said terms frelye and at ther pleasure spredd ther netts, byld ther lodges and capstynes and launch ther shyppes, crayers and bots, and to make docks for them to lye in at ther pleasures, not hurtful unto the said Barons, portsmen and inhabitants..' all of which indicates the importance of the fishing trade in Hythe at the time. Also reserved were 'commodities rysynge and comynge' out of the haven.

In Edward Cressye's lease the words referring to the stade need to be carefully considered. The precise location of St Clere's (or Cleere's) is uncertain, but does appear to have been either a piece of land or a small religious building, a church or chapel perhaps, situated in the vicinity of modern day Mackeson Court. *(End Map)* St Clere's was frequently mentioned in Corporation Assembly Minutes until the land was sold in 1664. The space between St Clere's and the 'Chapple of the Towne' can only mean the land between St Clere's and St Leonard's Church; but the words 'and so to the Stade' can scarcely mean that a stade lay beyond the parish church. The inference is that there was a second area of grazing land between St Clere's and the shore. Would such land have included the place now called The Green? The author would like to think so, and also suggests that the stade mentioned in Edward Cressye's lease was the 'old stade' referred to in the sources.

Some idea of the condition of the haven or harbour in the time of Edward Cressye in 1570 can be inferred from a number of late 16th century references to the harbour at Hythe, and these will now be considered. *(Front Map)*

On 10th March 1574, a grant was made to Martyn Allynson, miller. Two pieces of the 'Townes Lands' containing one acre (more or less) were allowed to Martyn Allynson whereone 'to set make and buylde a water myll uppon scituate and lyinge in the sayd Towne whereof one peece doth bound to the sayd channell goinge upp to the haven besyde the Shoemakers brydge weste to the Towne dike north and to the Towne lande east and south and the other peece dothe bounde to the sayd Channell easte to the highe waye weste to the Towne dike and the sayd Shoemakers brydge north and to the sayd Townes land south with the streams bancke and water courses to a water myll ptynyge or of right belonginge .' In modern words, that reads:-

"to set make and build a water mill upon situate and lying and being in the said town whereof one piece bounds to the channel going up to the haven beside the Shoemakers bridge west to the Town Dyke north and to the Town land east and south and the other piece bounds to the said channel east, to the highway west, to the Town Dyke and the said Shoemaker's bridge north and the said Town land south with the streams bank and water courses to a water mill appertaining or of right belonging." (See Front Cover)

The rent was to be 6s.8d. a year for the first ten years and then to be 10s. a year. No set time for the possession seems to have been agreed but the matter was to be referred for legal advice when the mill was built and working.

In addition, the Mayor etc. covenanted that it should be lawful for Martyn Allynson to make and set up two floodgates in the Town Dyke 'ryghte ageynst the end of the lande comynge from the conduit.' For his part, Martyn Allynson covenanted that he would 'when neede shall require beare mayneteyne and kepe the said Town dyke from the Weste brydge all alonge to the easte channel.'

The plans to build a water mill must have been carried out, for on 8th February 1580 the following was recorded:-

> *'Then at the same time Martyn Allynson because he dothe annoye the passage at the West bridge bye the stoppeinge of the water for his myll and to the hurte alsoe of the sayd brydge and decaye thereof by reason of passage and ryddinge over the said brydge hathe agreed and given his prmyse (promise) before us the sayd Mayor Jurats and Commons that he within one year next comynge wyll cause to be made and set uppon bye the sayd West brydge one brydge of stone and timber for caryage and passe over the same and other passage and to have in yt one arch of xii foote in wydness and after the same the fynyshinge thereof the sayd Martyn Allynson doth bynde him and his heyres to keep the reparacons (repairs) of the same stone brydge soe longe as he and his heyres doe possess and enioye the sayd myll and that the sayd Mayor Jurats and Commons have consented to allow hym towarde the same charge and worke three dayes worke of the whole Towne to be ordered bye the Surveyors of the Towne for the tyme beinge.'*

It seems that the damming of a stream to provide a head of water for Martyn Allynson's mill, and the resulting loss of a fording place, caused problems at the West bridge, both in structural damage and extra wear and tear due to the increasing use of the bridge by horses and carts displaced from the ford.

The Town Dyke mentioned in the arrangements made with Martyn Allynson is a clue to the location of the water mill. The Dyke or ditch is clearly marked on the Tithe Map of 1842 and included in the Schedules to the map. The water mill was clearly built some distance inland from the foreshore, in the vicinity of the present Rampart Road or the northern end of Oaklands, *(Maps Middle and End)* and the reference to a channel 'going up to the haven' suggests that a channel ran from the mill towards the seashore.

In February 1580, the Corporation agreed upon duties, in the sense of financial charges, for various commodities passing through the harbour. Such items included mackerel, herrings, salt, wheat, and other grains. In the same year the Mayor, Jurats and Commons also agreed to call a meeting of inhabitants of Hythe and West Hythe for the purpose of discussing the prospects of altering the 'maltod of the Towne.' The maltod or maltote seems to have been a long standing method of raising money, by means of a charge levied as a tax or impost upon the value of goods traded by the Town's businessmen. A shoe maker would pay 2s.2d. 'for his art', a merchant paid either 2d. or 4d. in the £1 on the value of merchandise traded, and a grazier or farmer paid 1d. for a cow sold, or 1/4d. for a hog sold, and so on.

Two years later, in February 1582, John Hasselhurst was allowed to gather the duties and profits of the haven and stade, and was required to render an account of the money received. For his pains he was allowed to have 3s.4d. in every £1 which he gathered, and the record shows that he collected £9.13s. 2d. In 1585, John Hasselhurst's 'commission' at the haven was 2s. in the £1 and at the stade 3s.4d. in the £1. In subsequent years up to 1589, the sums collected varied from £8.2s.2d. to £28.17s. 5d.

It is not easy to translate the sums of money quoted in old documents into modern terms. As a brief passing comment, the total income of the Corporation of Hythe in the year 1579 - 80 was £86.15s.1d. It is also apparent from these documents that even people with little command of the written word were able to make a respectable attempt at expressing figures when it came to money matters.

In 1587 the following decree was made:-

> "*At which Assembly also Daniel Langdon made peticon (petition) to them to graunte hym licence to buld a stoer howse at the hoye uppon the townes ground conteyning in length liii foote and in breadth xxiiii foote to be holden of them in ffee ffarme. The which they have graunted unto hym he paying for the same at the feast of the byrth of our Lord God yearly two shilling of lawful money of England to the Chamberlaynes of the sayd towne for the tyme being*".

Daniel Langdon's 'stoer howse' (a store house) at the 'hoye' will feature again in a subsequent chapter. *(Front Map)*

In the same year, 1587, on the 2nd February, a lengthy decree appears, again concerned with the charges at the haven. Once more, the person required to collect the charges was John Hasselhurst, stated to be Common Sergeant (or Town Sergeant) and to render a quarterly account for the monies received. A 'foreigner' shipping a mare or a jade was to pay 1s. per animal, and a freeman was to pay only 6d., half the amount. A jade was a horse in poor condition. Each foreigner taking merchandise overseas was required to pay 4d. for each 'C weight', presumed to mean a hundred weight, possibly then 100 lbs, and a freeman doing the same to pay only 2d. Every 'forryn Rippier that carryeth ffyshe for every seame' was to charged 1d., and again the freeman who was a rippier paid but half, namely 'ob' or 'obulus', the half penny. For 'every bote of the burthen of xv tonne and upwards passing oversea' there was 12d. or one shilling to be paid, and if the vessel was under 15 tons then only 6d. was to be paid. A shipwright 'that buyldeth a

newe bote or shipp within the town' was to be charged 12d. How many new boats were actually built is not revealed, but the 'seame' of fish in the time of King Richard the First (reigned 1189 - 1199) was a good horse load, and later equal to 8 bushels or 64 gallons, a considerable amount of fish.

In November 1588 an Assembly was held to discuss the cutting out of the haven. The phrase 'cutting out' occurs frequently in the sources used for this brief history. The phrase could mean either the clearing of a channel or waterway, or more likely, the process of making a way or passage from an existing channel to the sea. This seems to have been the meaning at Sandwich, where attempts to maintain the use of the harbour involved making a 'cut' or channel from the river Stour to the sea.

At Hythe, surveyors for the work of cutting out were chosen, and the townspeople were called to work at the haven, half of them on one day, the others on another day, according to the decision of the surveyors. Anyone unable to attend was obliged to send a deputy, and those who did not comply with the arrangements risked being committed to prison.

An Assembly for the 9th July 1591 produced the following decree, here rendered into modern language:-

> *"At which Assembly also it is Decreed that whereas there is a composition as made and agreed upon between the Worshipful Mr Thomas Scott Esquire and the township for the haven and sullage which is within the said Mr Scott's Liberty That he shall have yearly during the time that the haven is in his liberty two barrels of white herrings and 200 of red herrings which heretofore has been paid Whereupon he has (in consideration of the said herring) promised that the said township and their inhabitants shall have free egress in and to the said haven without any other tax for sullage to be paid for the same since which time the occupiers of the said lands have and do restrain the inhabitants of the said town to carry and recarry their necessary provisions to and from the said haven by reason whereof it is thought good that Mr Mayor and Mr Collens is chosen by this Assembly to repair to the said Mr Thomas Scott to receive his answer therein and according thereto to do as upon further advice they shall think good in the mean time."*

I think - at low tide from the slow moving water channels sand or shingle would have been dredged. (sullege)

They would use small stade boats to collect it in after going down to scoop it up. It would then be dumped on the banks for use in brickmaking, or shingle ballast

This decree would have identified the site of the haven if it had included the location of the Liberty of Mr Thomas Scott, which is unfortunately omitted. A possible position for Mr Scott's Liberty based on other evidence, is indicated on the front map.

There is documentary evidence of continuing attempts to keep the harbour open in the early 17th century. In 1615 a decree had been made for the cutting out of the haven and money collected for that purpose. In 1618 Thomas Wallop was called upon to give an account of all the monies he had received by virtue of the decree of December 1615 for the cutting out of the haven. In 1619, on the fourth of January, a decree was made for a similar purpose.

In the formal and legalistic language of the Minutes, the record states that 'At the said Assembly it is ordered and decreed that the Haven shall, with all convenient speede, be cut oute at such places as Mr Maior and the Jurates of this Towne, who are by this Assembly commissionated and authorized to see the said work done, shall think meete.' The spelling 'Mr Maior' in that passage is often used in early documents; the word usually means 'Mayor', but sometimes means 'major' as in 'maior part of voices' meaning a majority vote.

The Minutes continue with an assertion that the charges and labour of the work to be done should be borne by the people of every 'particular ward and place within the libertie of this Towne and Porte, according as they are charged and set downe in a Booke nowe at this tyme agreed uppon, for the better effecting of which worke every person appointed to labour therein is enjoyned to bringe with him (at the days and tymes by the said Commissioners to be appointed) a sufficient scuppet, shovel, mason's hod or small basket, and if any person charged with the said works doe refuse to worke or doe not send able men to worke for them and in their steede in such manner as in the said Booke is contayned then every person in suche case makeinge default shall forfaite and lose for every man not comeinge to labor in the said worke, or adjudged an insufficient labourer, for every day 12d. to be paid immediately to the Townsman .' The decree continued to say that if the forfeit was not paid to the Townsman, (or Town Sergeant) then a distress would be levied against the goods of the defaulter, and failing a sufficiency of his goods, then he could be sent to prison.

The haven was evidently still usable in 1623, for in that year Reginald Everinge accounted for 'moneys received uppon the Extracts ffor the duetyes of the haven and Stade for poundages' in the sum of £1.2s.8d.

The financial pressures connected with the need to save the harbour are frequently in evidence in the surviving record. In 1624 a petition had been sent to 'Our Honorable the Lord Warden' concerning the levying of a subsidy of tonnage towards the 'amending and newe makeinge of the haven and harborough of this Towne.' The Lord Warden answered by directing his petitioners to apply to Parliament for relief. In 1627, an Order was made that all persons who had formerly 'payd any money towards the effecting or obtaining of haven here which are since that time dead or removed their dwelling out of this Town shall absolutely lose the said moneys in regard of the manifold great impositions and burdens lately imposed and put upon the Inhabitants which now reside among us.' The 'impositions and burdens' at that time may well have been the demand for Ship Money coming from the King.

Chapter III
The Hoye

NOS. 116-120
Hall House 1580-1640

The source documents relating to the former harbour at Hythe mention, from time to time, not only the harbour or haven, but also the stade, the sluice, and the hoy, or 'hoye' in old spelling. A number of sources which mention the hoye will now be considered.

Although there are various definitions of the word 'hoye', for example as a type of ship, in a document of 1603 it is clear that the meaning of the word in Hythe at that time was a piece of land and also a building constructed upon that land.

The hoye is mentioned in the counterpart of a lease, dated January 1st 1603, by means of which the three sons of Daniel Langdon, a deceased merchant of Hythe previously mentioned, received from the Corporation a fee farm grant of lands. The grant included a piece of the Corporation 'batcheland' (beach land) commonly called the Hoye, being fifty five feet in length, and twenty five feet in breadth ('feet' being described as of His Majesty's Assize) upon which land 'the aforesaid Daniel Langdon in his lyfe tyme did build a store likewise commonly called the Hoye lyeing, standing and being in the Liberty of the Town and Port of Hethe aforesaid to a watercourse there commonly called the Common Channel against the East and South and to the other of the Town's batche lands aforesaid against the West and North.' The permission given to Daniel Langdon to build his 'stoer howse' in 1587 has been noted in a previous chapter, and the position of the building, at the south end of the harbour channel is shown on the middle map.

Further points mentioned in the grant to the sons of Daniel Langdon can be followed by consulting the middle map. There are references in the document to a piece of land called the Taynter, containing by estimation one acre 'lyeing and being' within the Liberty of the Town and Port of Hythe 'neare a certayne bridge called the Showmakers bridge' and 'to a certyne foote waye leading or going from the said bridge downe towards the Hoye aforesaid North and East and to a Common Carrying Waye there leading or going downe to the Hoye aforesaid towards the West.' If 'Showmakers bridge' was the same structure frequently mentioned in the Assembly Minutes under the name Shoemakers bridge, then the location was near the modern day Stade Street canal bridge, for that is the locality where the Shoemakers bridge seems to have been situated.

The Taynter, of about one acre, lay near the Shoemakers Bridge, and a footway leading from the bridge to the Hoye passed along the northern and eastern boundaries of the land. To the west of the Taynter lay a common carrying way, also going down to the Hoye. It is a reasonable assumption that these very direct routes enabled the convenient movement of goods by cart, horse or pack carrier between the town and the Hoye. The present day Stade Street possibly follows the course of the old common carrying way.

It is possible to infer from the wording of the grant to Daniel Langdon's heirs that in 1603, a water way described as the 'Common Channel' followed a course near the east and south of the 'Hoye', whilst to the west and east were 'batche' or beach lands belonging to the Corporation. The construction of the Royal Military Canal through Hythe involved the destruction of many of the features just described, and the 'Taynter' probably disappeared at that time.

The construction of the Royal Military Canal through Hythe involved the destruction of many of the features just described, and the 'Taynter' probably disappeared at that time.

Documents from the 17th century throw considerable light on what was happening on the Hythe foreshore. These sources can be seen against the background of events in the time of Charles I, Oliver Cromwell, and the eventual Restoration of Charles II in 1660. The effect of such political upheavals upon the lives of members of the Corporation of Hythe and their families is not evident from the surviving records, but it is clear that the membership included supporters of both Royalist and Parliamentary points of view. Although there are frequent references to people by name in the source documents, in many cases nothing further is known about persons who must have been prominent citizens in their time. However, it is possible to add a little detail about some of the people in the story.

In January 1625, Sir Peter Heyman and Mr Dixwell were elected to be Barons in Parliament for Hythe, and Mr Dixwell is recorded as having taken the oath sworn by other Barons to the Parliament for the maintenance of the Charters etc. excepting only his private interests and title at Folkestone. Mr Dixwell, was created a baronet after serving as Sheriff of Kent in 1626. As Sir Basil Dixwell, he began the building of Broome Park, Denton, on the road from Folkestone to Canterbury, and was related to John Dixwell, one of the signatories to the warrant for the execution of Charles I.

In 1629 the Corporation negotiated with Sir Basil Dixwell 'knight and Barronett' for the grant of a right of 'a free way or passage on his slipe or saults lying neare up to the towne of Hethe with carts or other carriages whatsoever made to the Maior, Jurats and Commonalty of Hethe aforesaid and their Successors unto the Haven belonging to the said towne and Porte of Hethe and we from tyme to tyme and at all tymes to alter our way as the sayd haven by reason of the abandon of beach shall alter without any manner of molestation, contradaxon or deniall.'

In 1628-29, he gave permission to the inhabitants of the Town at all times to come and go and carry goods over his land called the slipe at the east end of the Town, then in the occupation of Mrs Scott, without payment. In his 19th century book 'The Barons of the Cinque Ports,' George Wilks comments 'the right of way thus granted is the present Twiss Road'.

Hythe from the East. Drawn by L. Glennell pub. 1814.

The tilled bank hides the Millstream. The windmill (left) stands on the Corporation Innings. The nearer spit is Town Land with the East Bridge behind. On p 35 the same windmill is seen from above the church..see M.map.

The area of land referred to as Sir Basil Dixwell's slipe appears to have been the land between Twiss Road and Seabrook, in the 17th century a salt marsh. This area, at the east end of the town, is shown on the middle map. The land later formed part of the estate of the Honywood family with whom it remained for some considerable time. *(see illustration p24)*

The most likely position for the right of way granted by Sir Basil Dixwell was along the line of modern day Twiss Road which, in the 17th century, was probably the position of the Corporation's wall to the eastern side of the New Innings.

Quite why the Corporation needed a right of way along the slipe is not clear, since, in 1629, they owned most of the land which, at the time of writing, is occupied by the Council Recreation Grounds, the Premises of the Hythe Cricket Club, the remaining Twiss Road allotment gardens, and Fisher and Cobay Closes. Why not make a way across their own land - unless that meant building and maintaining bridges to span water channels. That would have meant spending money!

The middle map is based upon documents which come mainly from the later part of the 17th century. The 'Common Channel' mentioned in the grant to the heirs of Daniel Langdon can be seen as a waterway, fed by two freshwater streams and providing a passage from the sea to the town, eventually blocked by the construction of a sluice, an event shortly to be described in this account.

One of the documents provides further details of events close to the foreshore. In 1677 the Corporation agreed with John Terry, a carpenter of Hythe, to demise, grant and farm let, "all those their Outlands and Beachy Lands lying within the Liberty of the said Towne (that is to say) from the Maine Channel at the hoy and so over the puller of Beach as the other side of the said Channel to the stade and so to the West bridge westwards and along the common highway so farr their utmost bounds do lye and which was lately letten unto Thomas Strood of Hythe aforesaid But then and since were and now are in the occupacon of the said John Terry".

The wording of John Terry's lease is far from clear, especially as to the extent of the lands involved, and as to the meaning of the words 'westbridge westward' which seem particularly ambiguous. The middle map shows what may have been the situation at the time, and the end map will assist in relating the features to present day Hythe. It seems certain that the Green was included in John Terry's lease. The West bridge is thought to have been in the region of Red Lion Square and Thomas Hill's map of the lands of St Bartholomew's Hospital shows a structure labelled 'Hithe Bridge' crossing 'running water' at the approximate position of Red Lion Square.

Moreover the Hospital map shows the confluence of this 'running water' with a stream coming in from the east, (which we now call the Mill stream) the two streams combining to form a channel running southward towards a place marked a 'Stade Hoiye', at which locality the common channel enters the sea. This channel may well be the watercourse of a similar name mentioned in the abuttments of the Langdon lease of 1603. The road from 'Hithe Bridge' is shown going westwards to 'Galons (or Calons) Corner', a name bearing a suggestive similarity with the place now called Gallows Corner at the junction of the modern Dymchurch Road and the Scanlons Bridge Road. Also shown on Thomas Hill's map is 'The Road from Dimchurch' which, presumably, led

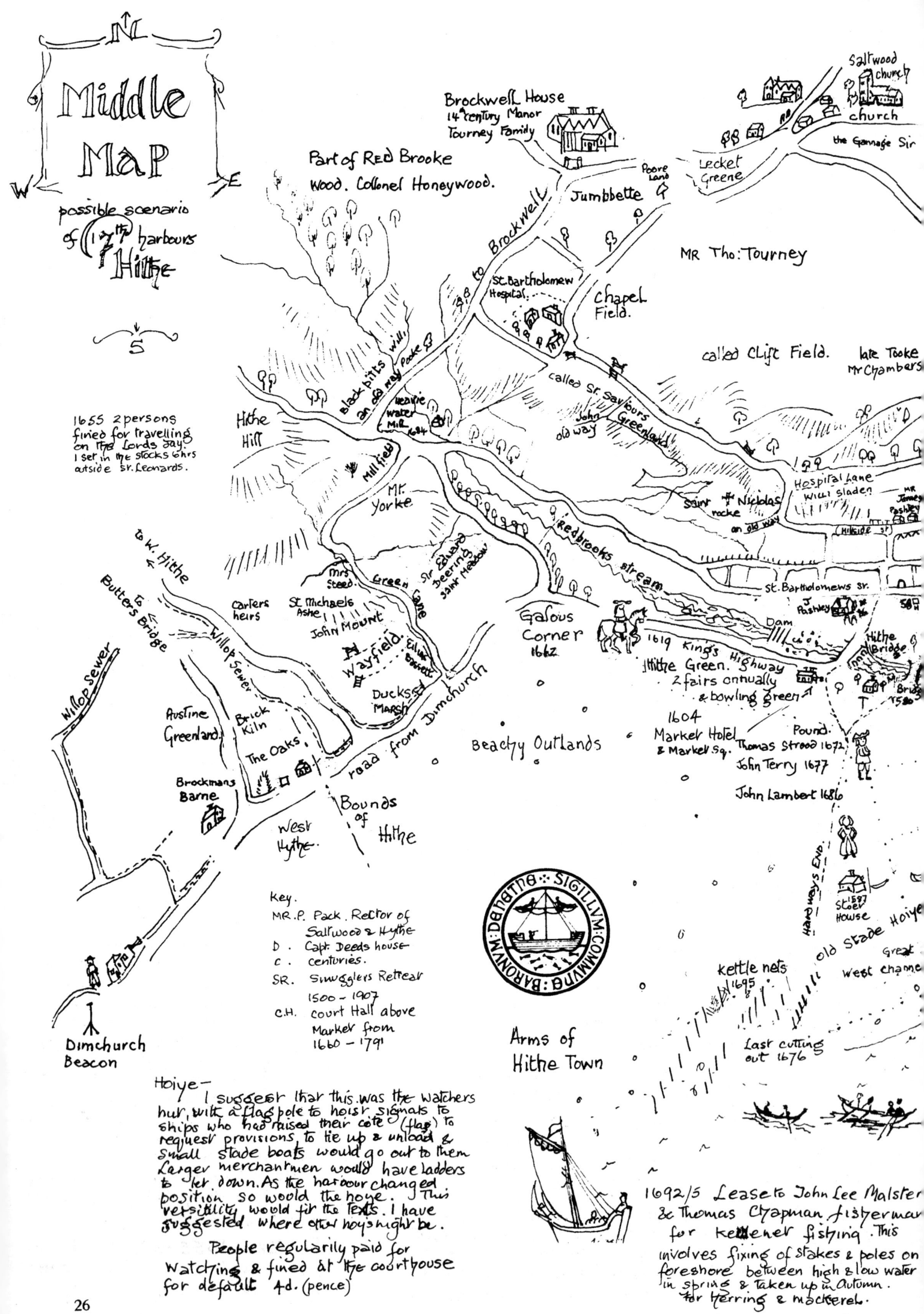

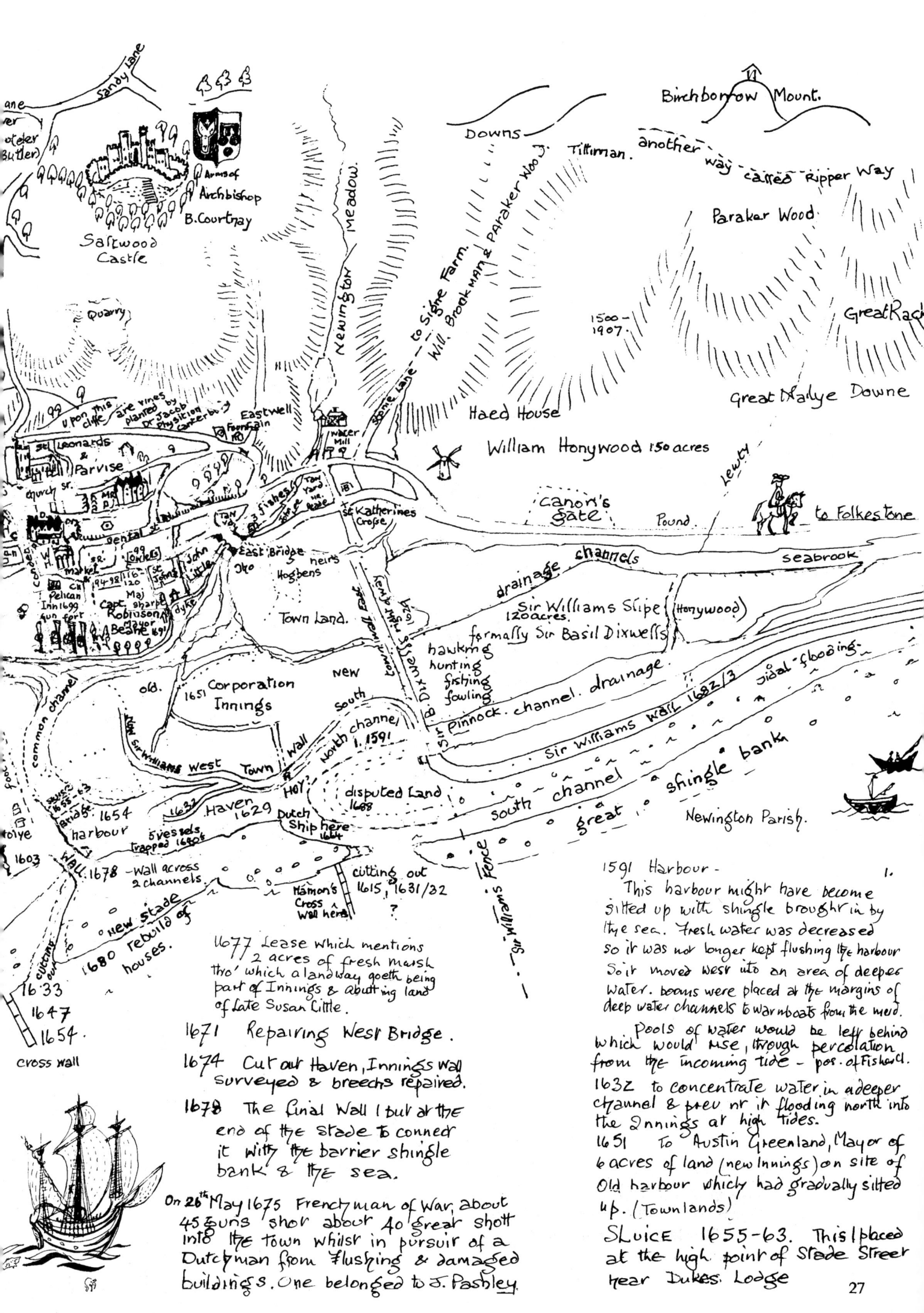

to and went towards the 'bounds of West Hithe'. It seems likely that the lands leased to John Terry were bounded by a line running south to north along the line of what is now Stade Street to the modern day Red Lion Square, and thence westward along the road to Dymchurch as far as the Grand Redoubt. Thus land now between Stade Street and St Leonard's Road, plus the Green and the Ranges, was included. The rent reserved for that sizeable tract of land was £16.10s. per year for the first two years, and then £14 per year for the remaining five years.

(see map of 1769, p48)

The present author's interpretation of the Langdon and Terry leases is that the Common Channel in 1603 was the channel carrying the waters of the two freshwater streams towards the sea. At the time of writing, these two streams, named the Brockhill stream and the Mill stream, flow into the Royal Military Canal at Scanlon's Bridge and Twiss Road Bridge respectively. The Main Channel at the hoy, spoken of in the Terry lease, was likely the southern channel which ran, roughly speaking, parallel with the foreshore, and is taken for this account to have led not only to the hoy but also to the haven. In the Langdon lease this channel seems to have been called 'common' at both the east and southern sides of the hoy.

The wording of a lease to John Lambert, dated 10th May 1686, is similar to that of the lease to John Terry in 1677. John Lambert was a victualler, and to him the Corporation leased 'all those their Outlands, Beachy Lands lying within the Libtie (i.e. Liberty) of the said Towne, that is to say ffrom the Maine Channel at the Hoy and soe over the puller of Beach at the other side of the said Channel to the Stade and soe to the West Bridge and along the Comon Highway towards Romney Marsh soe farr as their utmost bounds doe lye which were heretofore demised to Thomas Strode since to John Terry and are now in the occupacon of the said John Lambert or his assigns.'

In both the Terry and the Lambert leases the Corporation reserved the holding of the two fairs annually. The words of John Lambert's lease indicate that the two fairs were held between the West Bridge and the 'house where Stephen Weekes now dwelleth.' At the time of John Terry's lease the two fairs yearly were held anywhere upon the Green. The lease to John Terry also reserved for the use of the Corporation the Common Pound upon the Green. The Pound seems to have been close to the present day site of the British Legion Club premises at the northern end of St Leonard's Road. (End *Map*) The lease also reserved free way and passage to and from the bowling green, then railed in, without indicating precisely where the bowling green was situated.

Quoting further from John Lambert's lease:-

"Except and allways reserved out this present demise and lease unto the said Mayor, Juratts and Commonalty.. free libertie for the building and keeping of Two ffairs yearly between the West Bridge and the house where Stephen Weekes now dwelleth and alsoe upon the Green where the Common Pound now standeth and alsoe the Bowleing Greene now rayled in with free way and passage to and from the same. And also the like libertie and passage to and from the Common Pound when and as often as need shall require dureing this demise. And also free libertie of ingresse, egresse and regresse for the ffisherman and other Inhabitants of the said Towne to dry their netts and doe their other lawful occasions and business and also to erect storehouses and make docks for their necessary use at any convenient place or places at the Stade or along the Maine Channel from the Stade to the Haven and soe to the Hoy at any time or times dureing this demise. And also Except all former leases and grants unexpired and all ffee ffarmes theretofore granted as well of the windmill late standing upon the said Outlands with two acres of beachy land thereto belonging, as divers houses and cottages standing upon part of the said Outlands and free libertie for the said Inhabitants to lay any Timber or Batts on any convenient place or places of the said Pound Greene and Likewise for Cattell and Carriages (bringing Comodeties to the said Towne) to sit and rest upon the said Greene without Lett or interruption of the said John Lambert."

There were other exceptions and reservations in Lambert's lease. Those included such beachy lands near the stade as might, during the term of the demise, be enclosed or built upon by any person.

John Lambert's lease points to the existence of a channel between the stade and the haven but is confusing as to relative location of the hoy. The wording of the lease seems to indicate that the hoy lay beyond the haven, but such a situation would be incompatible with the information to be gleaned from the grant of the right of way to the haven by Sir Basil Dixwell in 1628/1629. The intention may simply have been to ensure that fisherman and others would be able to use the foreshore on both sides of the channel as far as the haven and back again to the hoy. The author's view of the likely topography is shown in the middle map.

Chapter IV
Cutting Out

The Assembly Book for the period 1624 to 1635 contains a decree dating from sometime in 1631 or 1632 which tells of the intention to construct a 'crosse wall'.

The precise nature and purpose of the 'crosse wall' are a mystery, and the reference to the 'Stade' is also puzzling. Did that mean the 'old stade', the one thought to have been close to Fisherman's Beach, that is at the western end of the Great or West Channel? The 'crosse wall' was expressed to be near the hoy, but how near? The decree, with modernized spelling reads as follows:-

> *"Whereas the Haven belonging to the Town and Port of Hythe aforesaid is of late gone to decay and ruin and is wholly swarved up which is likely to turn to the great prejudice of this township unless some speedy course be taken therein, whereupon at this Assembly it is ordered that the Haven shall be cut out anew near the Stade as at the discretion of Mr Mayor of this town and the Jurats here shall seem convenient by the general contribution of every well disposed inhabitant of this town; and for the better maintenance and preservation of the said Haven being cut out aforesaid the fishermen of this town of their free voluntary will and pleasure have consented, and whereupon by this Assembly it is ordered and decreed, to make a half share of every fishing boat of all fishing voyages and other voyages whatsoever from the feast of the purification of St Mary the Virgin next come twelve month to make a cross wall near the hoy as formerly has been and for the more speedy effecting and making of the said cross wall, Lawrence Wellard did of himself freely assume and promise to this Assembly for the consideration of ten pounds of lawful money of England in hands paid to make a sufficient cross wall in breadth in the bottom 16 foot and the top 4 foot and he is to leave the said wall sufficient in every respect 12 months after the finish therof which ten pounds was promised to him by this House accordingly and he to go on with all convenient speed and the town is to authorise and are to gather the money coming by the half share aforesaid by the space aforesaid and the surplusage of the ten pounds coming thereby shall be deposited to and for the maintenance of the said cross wall after the said Lawrence Wellard has done therewith and he the said Lawrence to put in the bond of £20 to make and leave the wall sufficiently for the space above said, subpoena to repay the said twenty pounds if default made by him in cutting out the said Haven."*

In the next part of the decree, the Mayor and other persons were appointed surveyors of the work, and were made responsible for hiring workmen at their discretion.

Another decree soon followed, as recorded in the Minutes of 23rd March 1633.

> *Whereas the haven belonging to this Corporation of Hythe is at present absolutely stopped and swarved upp whereby noe boate or other vessell cann com in or out to the great inconvenience and impoverishment of this towne the promises being considered and the requests and desires of divers fishermen and inhabitants of this Towne made to Mr Maior and the Jurates of the Corporation craveing and desireing the sayd Mr Maior by an officer to summons and warne the whole body of the sayd Corporacon to a generall meeting whereby every guift or liberalitie of every freeman of this Towne for and towards the cutting out, opening and new makeing of the sayd Haven might appeare which hath been done accordingly and every freeman of this Towne hath promised to be contributorie concerning the premisses And for the better effecting of the same this Assembly holden the 23 day of March Anno Dmi. 1633 by the Maoir, Jurates and Commons and freemen in the Towne hall have elected and desired Mr John Crump and Mr Guy Langdon, Jurates and Christostum Grout and Richard Hogben Coiers, to repayer to every forrener inhabiting within this Towne (yt being a generall benefit likewise to take their liberalities and contributions in waiting for and towards the cutting out of the sayd haven which alsoe appeareth by several noates in writing under the hands of the sayd parties).*

> *Whereuppon at this Assembly yt is ordered and decreed that William Symons and William Gately shall speedily collect and gather of every freeman and forriner of this Towne the sayd guift, benevolence and liberalitie for and towards the sayd cutting, opening and new makeing of the sayd haven according to their several promises and to paye the same to James Pashley and Robert Curtis who have assured and taken uppon them the cutting out, opening and new makeing the sayd haven for the several guifts and contributions promised as aforesayd and yt is further ordered by the authority of the Assembly aforesayd that the sayd James Pashley and Robert Curtis shall presently enter into a bond of 30 li. to Mr George Reeve Maior to the use of this Corporacon for the performance of their promises before the first day of May next ensuing which is consented unto by the sayd parties accordingly."*

John Crump was a Jurat for twenty five years, and according to a note in the Minute Book at the time of his death, had never been Mayor, which must have been somewhat unusual. Guy Langdon and William Gately were both later to be Mayors, and the latter was also elected Bailiff to Yarmouth.

The closeness of these two decrees suggests that either they were made at a time when natural processes were interfering with the foreshore and the water channels leading into the haven, or perhaps that the cross wall mentioned in the decree of 1631 or 1632 was never constructed. In any event the earlier decree presents something of a puzzle since the hoy and the stade appear to have been fairly widely separated at that time. The Assembly Minutes for the period 1591 to 1608 have not survived, and it may be that there was a change in the position of the stade during those years. A further complication is that the Minute Book for the period 1624 to 1635 has been rebound at some time in its existence and has numerous blank folios. There is a possibility that the position of the harbour may have been changed from the Liberty of the Worshipfull Thomas Scott to the 'common channel' mentioned in the lease of 1603 to the sons of Daniel Langdon.

Reference was made in an earlier chapter to a decree of 1591 concerning an agreement between the Worshipful Mr Thomas Scott and the townspeople relating to free access to the haven over 'Mr Scott's Liberty.' Despite that decree, the Corporation Assembly Minutes indicate that in general, attempts to save the haven were carried out on land under the control of the Mayor and Corporation. There is little firm evidence of a need to obtain permission from any other person or body of persons. In 1641, however, a promise was made to one of the then Chamberlains that he would be secured for a bond of £20 entered into by him in favour of a person named Gibson who had evidently undertaken to procure a patent for the 'reparacon' of the haven. Unfortunately the outcome of the matter is not on record, for the Minutes of Assembly between 1641 and 1649 have not survived, possibly because those were the troubled years of the Civil War.

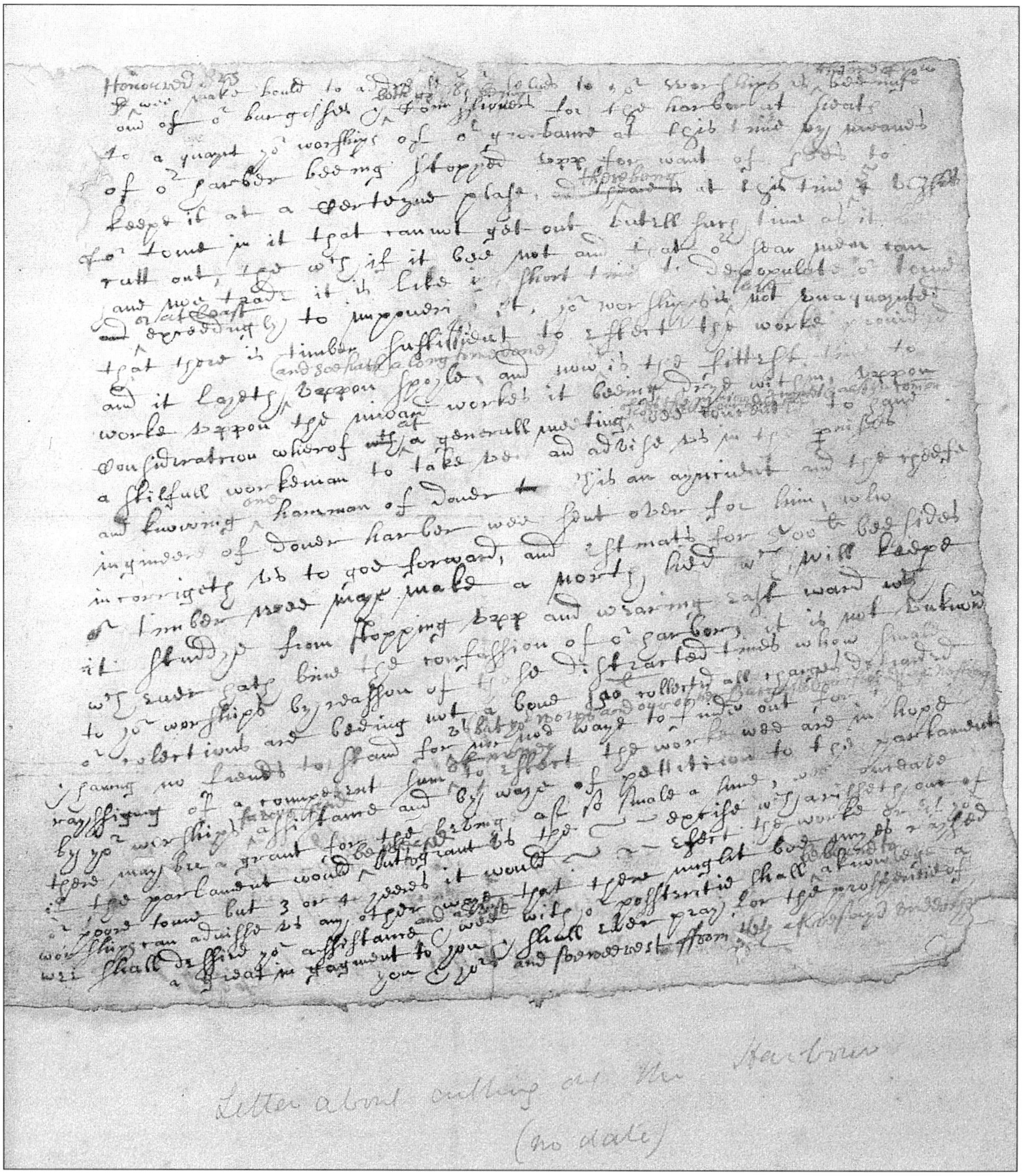

In general the Corporation's actions in relation to the haven were of a 'self help' nature, and the 'do it yourself' quality of the work can be inferred from the appointment of local people as 'surveyors and persons commissionated.' There is however, an item of evidence which suggests that at one stage, outside help was obtained. The document in question takes the form of a paper, pasted on to thin card, at the base of which are written the words 'Letter about the cutting out of the Harbour'. This Archive item appears to be a copy or draft of an undated letter bearing no indication of its intended destination. As a result, and because of the difficulty in reading scribbled and obscure words, only a limited reliance can be placed upon this document. It is nonetheless intriguing. In the following quotation, words in brackets represent the author's interpretation of obscure points. *(see previous page)*

"Honoured Sirs" the words begin, *"wee make bould to (address) to your worships as the one of you beinge one of our burgesses and both of you beinge commissioners for the harbour at Heath to acquaynt your worships of our (grievance) at this time by (means) of our harbour beeing stopped upp for want of (head) to keepe it (a) certain place, there beinge at this time 5 vessels of our towne in it that cannot get out untill such time as it bee cut out."*

The writer continued with a warning that failure to cut out the harbour would result in the seamen having 'noe trade' and that either depopulation or impoverishment of the town would result. Timber was available for the work to be done, and a 'skilful workman' had been called to advise the Corporation. He appears to have been a person by the name of Hamon, described as the 'cheefe inginiere' of Dover harbour, who possibly gave his name to 'Hamon's Head' shown on a plan of Dover Harbour dated 1616, and 'who incorrigeth us to go forward and estimate for £500 besides our timber.' Mr Hamon's idea seems to have been to make a mouth or head which would prevent shingle or silt from blocking the entry to the harbour and causing it to wear eastward which 'hath been the confusion of our harbour'.

One of the main concerns evident in Corporation Minutes of this period is the cost of trying to save the harbour. This document is no different. 'It is not unknown to your worships by reason of these distracted times when small collections are not above £100, of all charges defraid, so having no friends to stand for us (but your worships and our other burgesses)' are words which come to the core of the letter, and the closing words indicate that the senders wished to petition Parliament to 'grant us the excise which ariseth out of oure poore towne but 3 or 4 years it would effect the work.' Their worships were then asked, by way of an alternative, if they had any other advice to offer, and the final words, which degenerate into a cramped scribble, contain a hint or some sort of promise to 'your worships' that 'with our possteritie we shall be bound to acknowledge a great ingagement to you (and) shall ever pray for the prosperitie of you and yours.'

Further problems in this period are highlighted in a report by Mr H.W. Hewlett, adviser to the Crown in a 19th century dispute concerning the foreshore at Hythe. In the report, which appeared in newspaper articles of 1884/85, Mr Hewlett stated that in his inspection of Minutes dating from 1649, he noted an entry recording a sum of £9.3s.3d. paid to Elias Bassett when the haven was cut out in 1647. This entry suggested to Mr Hewlett that "what was done on this occasion, however, to clear the channel, must have been trifling and ineffectual, as the next entry on the subject is that of February 1654, attributing the decay of the town to the swarveing up of the haven and harbour and ordering that they shall be cut out."

Chapter V
The Sluice

The document relating to the state of the harbour referred to previously by Mr Hewlett was a Minute of Assembly dated 28th February 1654. It is clear from this Minute that members of the Corporation were seriously concerned about the effect on trade of the poor condition of the harbour at that time.

> *"This Assembly taking into consideration the great decay of this Towne in the want of trade whereby it is much impoverished and that the apparent ground or cause hereof is by Reason of the Swarveing up of the Haven and harbour belonging to the Towne Have ordered and decreed that the haven shalbee cut out with all convenient speede to which purpose the said Mayor Jurats and Commons have condiscended (and) agreed to contribute to the said works as followeth .'*

There then follows a note which says 'Mr Lushington, Mayor, 4000 of Wallstuffe to bedde at the sea-side', and then a table of the names and sums of money, ranging from five shillings to five pounds, which the various persons named had agreed to contribute. There is, however, a marginal note, signed Jo. Handfield, which reads 'Memd. of these somes there was never a penny ever paid'. (Memorandum, of these sums there was never a penny ever paid). John Handfield had been appointed Town Clerk on 25th January 1654, and resigned on 22nd November 1662, but remained until his successor Isaac Rutton was appointed. Quite what the Mayor's 'Wallstuff' was is not defined, but was possibly some material to shore up the beach whilst the 'cutting out' was in progress, with the intention of keeping the sea out of the working area. The Minute records that the Mayor was chosen to be one of the collectors of contributions towards the 'said Haven'.

For March 7th 1654 we read a somewhat curious entry :-

> *"Att this Assembly Edmund Beane, upon his proposition and engagement to give towards the Haven ten shillings more than any other ffisherman in this Towne should give (excepting Mr Elias Bassett and John Cheeseman), was admitted a ffreeman and thereuppon hee took the oath of a ffreeman accordingly".*

At the same Assembly Edmund Beane was elected a Common Councilman. These Minutes then continue:-

> *"The occasion of this Assembly being principally to consult of somewhat in order to the makeing of the Intended Haven It was put to the vote whether a Sluice should be made or not And it was resolved upon the question in the affirmative".*

> *"Afterwards it was concluded and agreed upon by this Assembly that one hundred pounds should be borrowed upon the security of the Townes Lands towards the buying of Timber Plancks, Iron and other Materialls for the makeing of the said Sluce".*

The words 'Intended Haven', which are to be found elsewhere in this chapter, suggest that a new harbour was contemplated in 1654, hence the suggestion for a change from the location of 1591.

Putting the cost quoted for materials into context, it is worth noting that in the currency of the day, the 'Total of all Receipts' for the year ended February 2nd 1654 was £130.8s.11d.

Some foreboding of troubles to come is perhaps contained in the following words, also from March 7th 1654:-

> *"Whereas at the Assembly holden the 28th day of ffebruary last sixe Surveyors were chosen for the buying of timber and overseeing of the worke of the haven, severall of which persons so elected were at the time of their eleccon absent from the Assembly who for certaine causes have since laid downe and resigned their places It is therefore ordered that nine others shalbe elected and appointed Surveyors for the surveyeing and appointing of the worke to bee done about the Sluce and cutting of the Haven ."*

The construction of a 'sluce', or in present spelling 'sluice', was an important part of attempts to keep the harbour open. As previously mentioned, Mr H.W.Hewlett was involved as adviser to the Crown in a 19th century dispute relating to the foreshore at Hythe. In his report at that time, he observed that the making of the sluice appeared to have absorbed the whole or the greater part of the money received. He thought the sluice to be a new artificial outlet for the freshwater streams and to be 'situate far above high water mark', presumably

Dover and Sandwich, the idea behind the construction of a sluice was to impound a good head of water which could be released when required, in order to flush out shingle or silt which was blocking a water channel or harbour basin. The author's opinion is that the most likely position for the sluice of 1654 was in the Common Channel flowing past the hoy. In a later chapter, George Wilk's newspaper articles of 1884 and 1885 are discussed. In those articles, another opinion about the entrance to the harbour was put forward, suggesting that it was near Martello Tower Number 13, now converted into a private residence on the West Parade.

Some support for the use of a sluice as a device for impounding a head of water is to be found in a Minute of the 24th April 1656:-

> "Att this Assembly Peter Johnson, for the consideration of £5 by the year did undertake to the looking to the sluce, drawing up and letting down the gates for one yeare, to and at Candlemas next And in case any damage or wrong should happen to the sluce, channel or harbor by or through his neglect Peter Johnson did oblige himself to make reparacon".

There is also a Minute of somewhat obscure meaning dated 12th June 1657 which says:-

> "Ordered that Thomas Fordred bee sluce keeper till Candlemas next And in case the full doe not breake so that the sluce may bee kept going then the said Thomas is to have £4 for keeping Otherwise if the said full doe breake out then he is to have onely three pounds".

Thomas Fordred was re-appointed sluice keeper on 2nd February 1658.

Returning to the theme of costs, the 'letter about cutting out of the Harbour', already mentioned, indicated that the Corporation had timber available for the making of a sluice, but an Assembly of 9th April 1654 was informed that James Brockman Esq. required security for the money due to him for timber purchased for work at the harbour, and Mr Weller and Mr Grenland agreed to be bondsmen for the payment of the money, they in their turn to be secured by the Corporation out of the rental of a piece of land in the occupation of John Bassett.

In those days the principal source of income for the Corporation derived from the letting and leasing of land and buildings owned by the Corporation which formed an extensive portion of the Liberty of the Town and Port of Hythe.

A further example of borrowing money against the security of land appears from a Minute of the 9th April 1655 which reads:-

> "Att this Assembly it was further ordered that the peece of land in the occupacon of Widow Littlewood containing .. acres shall bee made over to John Cheeseman for the security of £100 Borrowing of him for and towards the making of the Intended Haven in such manner as the mortgage to Capt. Deedes for security of £100 was made And that Mr Handfield doe make the same accordingly."

John Cheeseman had been one of the two named surveyors for the work at the haven, and another surveyor had been Phillip Littlewood, husband, perhaps, of Widow Littlewood.

Economy was also in the thoughts of the Corporation, for at their Assembly on the 9th April 1655 they ordered that 'the chips and fuel arising from the timber cut out for the making of the sluce etc. shall bee from time to time sold by one of the severall surveyors of the worke and the moneys from thence arising to bee accounted unto this house'.

On May 21st 1655 the 'nine surveyors before elected' were dismissed from their places and it was voted and agreed that one Expenditor should be chosen for the 'manageing of the work of the haven which Expenditor so chosen should bee allowed xiid. per diem for his services for every day that he should be imployed in the said sluce.' Mr Austen Grenland was chosen to be that expenditor and to receive the twelve pence per day. In addition Mr Grenland was to be allowed another twelve pence per week for the cost of a clerk to 'cost up and transcribe his accounts concerning the said work.'

At this time, in 1654 and 1655, possibly due to the state of the harbour, there seem to have been more frequent meetings of the Corporation, as can be seen from an Assembly Minute dated 21st June 1655:-

> "Whereas there hath lately beene and will bee multiplicity and diversity of business to be concluded on about the ordering and appointing of the work of the Sluce in order to the erection of the intended Haven whereby the house is necessitated to meete often to the great trouble of severall persons whose negotiations are urgent. In consideration whereof this Assembly have thought fitt to authorise and commissionate severall persons to bee Trustees on the behalf of this House to act Decree and order at all and convenient places, times and seasons touching the manageing of the affairs of the said Haven as fully and effectually to all intents purposes as if such act or decree of such Trustees to bee chosen or the greater number of them should bee the proper act and decree of this House and this power and authority invested into them to continue untill the same shalbe repealed by order from this House and no longer."

This Minute seems to be telling us that the private business of Corporation members was being interrupted by the need to call Assemblies, and so they decided to appoint trustees to have the power to act on behalf of the Corporation. The same Assembly decided to authorize the borrowing of a further sum of £200 for the haven project.

> "Whereas there is urgent occasion for the use of more moneys towards the manageing of the work of the Sluce and Haven It is therefore putt to the question how much money should bee taken up for the present towards the said charge and by the greater number of voices it was agreed upon that two hundred pounds more bee speedily borrowed upon the Townes security. And whereas Mr Zouch Brockman of Cheriton gent. is willing to furnish this house with £100 towards the worke of the haven upon security to bee given to him out of the Townes Lands. It is therefore ordered that the two pieces of the townes lands in the occupacon of John Gray and Peter Whitlock containing four acres part of the New Innings shalbee bound to the said Mr Brockman for security of the said moneys for one year."

The same Minute goes on to say that John Dove of Sandgate Castle, soldier, was willing to advance a further one hundred pounds, upon security to be made to him out of the Towns lands by means of a mortgage. For that purpose the Assembly ordered that a piece of land in the Old Innings and occupied by John Bassett should be mortgaged to John Dove as a security for his loan, and also that the rent on the land should be paid as interest on the loan for so long as the (loan?) remained outstanding.

The sums of money lent by Mr Brockman and John Dove were evidently soon spent, for a Minute, dated the 20th August 1655 has this to say:-

> "Whereas Mr Grenland made complaint to this House that the moneys which were taken up upon the Towns security of Mr Brockman and Mr Dove is well nigh expended and that there will bee sudden neede of more moneys It is therefore with one generall consent ordered and decreed That one hundred pounds more be taken up upon the townes security towards the worke of the Haven and that it bee referred to the six Referees to assigne security out of the Townes lands to such persons as will lend the same".

Attempts were made at this time to raise money from sources further afield. The Minutes for the 21st June 1655 recorded that a decision had been taken for a 'peticon', i.e. a petition, to 'bee drawne up' and presented to the 'Brotherhood and Guestling for a collection through the Ports and Limitts towards the intended Haven and for their assistance to promote the Adres (Address?) to His Highness the Lord Protector'. The order presenting a petition to the Lord Protector, Oliver Cromwell, was made on the 20th August 1655, but the subsequent Minutes do not, unfortunately, record the response.

1655 2 persons fined for travelling on Lord's Day. 1 set in stocks 6 hours. The stocks were outside St. Leonards.

On a more practical and realistic footing Mr Grenland, Expenditor, asked for an assistant to deputize for him when he was away, and Laurance Weller was appointed to that position. Laurance Weller was a Jurat of Hythe, and his forename is also written as Lawrence, with the surname appearing variously as Weller, Wellerd or Wellard. In addition to his involvement with the harbour, Laurance Weller seems to have been a local benefactor, and by his will he created a Hythe Charity in 1663. The benefit of a piece of land in Saltwood, and the interest on a sum of money of £80, were to be used in putting poor children of widowed mothers to apprenticeship; and if none such could be found, the Churchwardens and Overseers could so benefit poor children whose parents were in 'no waie' (no way) able to provide for them.

Further examples of the financial pressure resulting from attempts to save the harbour are seen in a Minute for September 30th 1655, when land occupied by Ferdinando Bassett and Elias Bassett was pledged as a security for the sum of £100 needed to pay the workmen who had 'cut out the haven'; and a house was to be sold to the tenant, Bartholomew Lee, for the sum of £30, the money to be used to pay the workmen in arrears. Unlike most of the characters in this story, in the case of Ferdinando Bassett, there are a few extra details about him in the records. In 1648, he purchased

The White Hart in Hythe High Street from Henry Hart of Stone Hill, Sellindge, and by his will, he created a series of life interests in the property, which lasted until a descendant Elias Bassett, broke the succession after the death of his brother John Bassett of New Romney. The White Hart Inn was then sold to Julius Deeds in 1734/35. The surname Bassett is sometimes thought to be linked with a survivor of the Spanish Armada, but there is also a suggestion that the name had Huguenot origins. Variant spellings are Bassock or Bassooke. Ferdinando Bassett's name was added to the list of trustees who managed the work at the harbour.

The Minutes of Assembly for 30th September 1655 include the following item:-

> *"Ordered that the present Chamberlains and John Cheeseman doe comply and agree with such persons as will buy any of the Townes houses for the sale of them and doe make report therof at the next meeteinge".*

Shortly before, on September 5th, security was given to Richard Rosse, of Dovor (i.e. Dover) for £100 borrowed of him for five years. The security was land in the occupation of William Fordred and Peter Philpott.

The Corporation Assembly on 2nd February 1655 suffered a dramatic interruption on the arrival of a visitor.

> *"Captain Knott of Sandgate Castle accompanied with several of his soldiers entered the Common hall and produceing the late Proclamation of his highness prohibiting delinquents to bear office or to have any voice or vote in the eleccon of any publique officer Did then charge the most part of this Corporation to bee included within the said Proclamation affirming that the treasonable engagement in the said Proclamation mentioned was the petition of Kent in 1648: Whereupon also the said Captain Knott did charge several particular persons in the Assembly with delinquency refusing to depart the house as long as those parties whom hee did so charge continued their places. And then some of the Comoners to witt John Graye and John Mercer did depart the house and one of the ffreemen to witt Stephen Binge alsoe. Mr Grenland and Mr Woolball continued their places but refused to vote; and the said Captain Knott continued in the Assembly".*

Captain Knott's intrusion occurred during the Commonwealth period, and subsequent entries indicate similar intrusions by other persons after the Monarchy was restored under Charles II.

The efforts to save the harbour did not however come to an end, for in April 1656, shortly after Captain Knott's visitation, more of the Town's property was to be sold to pay debts, and Thomas Kitchen lent the Corporation the sum of £40. Land in the occupation of Ferdinando Bassett was to be demised to Thomas Kitchen for 99 years as security for the loan. In January 1656 Thomas Kitchen paid £4 for the use of the Town's timber lift in the harbour, and judging from the Chamberlain's accounts he also paid 13s.4d. for the use of a windmill, suggesting that he was a miller by trade. The same accounts reveal that the sum of 1s.6d. was paid for 'beere the day the harbour was cut out'.

Following the Assembly of January 30th 1656, there was an order that 'all outlandish Merchants which hereafter shall come unto this harbour shall pay to the use of the Corporation for harbourage the some of 5s., ffishermen only excepted who shall pay but twelve pence for harbourage as aforesaid.'

The Corporation evidently had hopes of obtaining income from the harbour, for in addition to the order of January 1656, they also made another which read:-

> *"Att this Assembly the house rated the shipping of corne to bee transported from the port as followeth, ffor wheate, barley, mault, Rye, Beans, pease, oats and all other graine for ffreemen one penny the quarter, ffor wheate for fforeynors 4d. the quarter and for barley, mault, rye, beans, pease and oats and all other graine ffor fforeynors 3d. the quarter".*

Somewhat later, at the Candlemas Assembly in 1657, John Browning was confirmed in the office of Common Sergeant at Mace (i.e. of Town Sergeant) and was required to give an account to the Chamberlains of the monthly receipts of harbourage from Frenchmen and others during the 'present year ensuing'. Another entry for the 5th October 1658 also indicates that the Town Sergeant had the task of collecting the harbour dues.

> *"At this Assembly it was ordered that all the profits and sums of money payable for and arising from the harbour of this Towne now being and remaining in the Town Sergeant's hands and whatsoever shall hereafter arise or bee payable for the same shall bee imployed towards the keeping and repairing and maintaining thereof by Mr Elias Bassett and John Cheeseman, Surveyors of the same until further order of the Assembly".*

It is evident from documentary references that coal was part of the merchandise passing through the harbour at this time. In 1659, on 2nd February, Thomas Samon was elected 'meeter' and allowed 2d. per 'chalder' for coals imported. Thomas had the task of measuring the coals, possibly in a bushel basket, and collecting the dues. For his efforts he was allowed two pence per chaldron, a measure of volume now obsolete and which seems to have been variable from place to place. References tell of the Imperial chaldron of 32 bushels, and the Winchester chaldron of 36 bushels, but surviving documents indicate that there was a Hythe chaldron equal to one and a half Winchester chaldrons, i.e. 54 bushels. Coal dues continued to be a source of income until well into the 18th century, when they were assigned to the Hythe Commissioners of Pavement formed in 1798 under the Statute 38 Geo. 111 Chapter 16, the so-called Hythe Paving Act.

The "Three Brothers" - one of a fleet of colliers, owned by Joseph Horton, unloading coal at the Stade. These colliers plied between Hartlepool and Hythe, landing coal for the town at the Stade, and at the Gas Works beach. In winter, when Hythe beach was inaccessable, the coal was landed at Folkestone and transported by pony and cart to Hythe.
Harry Griggs was mate of the "Three Brothers", and Wright Griggs became mate of the "Vivid" at eighteen.

Although there were many efforts to keep the navigable channels open in the middle years of the 17th century, documentary evidence suggests that no lasting success was achieved, and there were increasing signs that the days of the harbour were numbered.

Chapter VI
Swan Song

After the middle of the 17th century, there are fewer references to the harbour in the Assembly Minutes. In July 1659 Mr. *(sic)* Honywood had offered to maintain the harbour and sluice for twenty one years for an annual rent of ten pounds, but the offer does not seem to have been accepted. In February 1662 the sum of forty shillings was due to Thomas Kitchen for looking after the sluice during the year ended February 1660.

Perhaps the approaching swan-song of the harbour is heard in November 1663, when we read that 'This Assembly hath appointed Mr Gray, Mr John Bassett and Mr Robinson Beane to sell the sluce house and such things about the sluce bridge as are necessary to be sold for the use of this house.'

Writing in the 19th century, Mr Hewlett, who has already figured in this account as Adviser to the Crown in a dispute over rights to the Hythe foreshore, concluded that silting of the channel had continued, so much so that in February 1674 another 'cutting out' was ordered. This work was evidently carried out in 1676. A note of finality, and a hint of the approaching end of the haven, appears in an order of 1678 to construct a wall across the channel at the Hythe sluice in order to make a stade. Mr Hewlett thought that statement implied making a wharf. Assuming the stade would need to be as close to the sea as possible, that order supports the notion of a sluice seaward of the fated harbour.

The records provide information about house building activities on the shore, and details about one of the characters involved. Sir Leoline Jenkins, Fellow of Jesus College Oxford, was knighted in 1670. At various periods he held important offices as a judge, Privy Councillor, Secretary of State, and Baron in Parliament for Hythe. In June 1671, Sir Leoline Jenkins had obtained permission to build houses at the stade upon payment of one penny per perch for such land as he might enclose, and in 1676 two entries refer to a feoffment by Lady Honywood of houses at the stade and to the spending of ten shillings for 'bread, Beer, meate and tobacco' when the Corporation received possession of houses. Were those houses the same ones erected by Sir Leoline Jenkins in 1671?

At that time, in 1676, the Assembly ordered that a house at the stade should be cleared of goods of the fishing trade. In 1677, the Corporation ordered that timber and material from the Town's houses that were lately 'fallen down' should be sold. The houses had evidently been undermined by the sea. Later, in 1680, the Minutes record that more houses were being built at the stade. *(End Map)*.

These brief fragments of information (and they are no more than that in the original documents) pose more questions than are answered, but they do give some hints of what was happening near the Hythe sea shore in the late 17th century. *(See Middle Map)*

The time has come to present an order and decree which the present author dubs 'the Shorncliffe decree', perhaps an epitaph for Hythe harbour. The date is July 1st 1679.

"*This Assembly haveing taken into consideration the sadd effects which have accrewed to this Corporation by cutting open the haven on or about the yeare 1676 whose natural course antiently was to worke towards the East by divers and sundry fallings away untill the issue or mouth of the said haven had its being att or neere a place called Shorncliffe but of late years since the cutting aforesaid hath inclined towards the west not only eat away the old Stade where captons and Boats use to be, but also the houses which were there built for the incouragement of ffishermen and the general benefit of this Towne to the great prejudice not only of the ffishermen but also of all others tradeing of this Town and Port We therfore the Mayor, Jurats and Commonalty of this Corporacon at this Assembly for the ease and encouragement of ffishermen and others tradeing of this Port have unanimously thought fitt and doe now order and decree that for the rebuilding of a new Stade neare the said Towne that a substantial wall be forthwith made crosse the two channels att or neere the place called the Sluce to the full next the sea and that Mr Elias Bassett, Phillip Bing and Peter Johnson be overseers of the said worke and have the management of the same and to render a true accompt thereof to this Corporacon upon oath and also that the Honorable Sir Edward Deering Bart. be acquainted with the necessity of the said worke and the benefit which may accrew to the Corporacon thereby and what his Honor would be pleased to doe towards the effecting the said worke.*"

Taking Shorncliffe as being in its present position to the east of Hythe, the 'antient' or ancient course was likely to be a channel running west from Seabrook towards Hythe, the 'sure gut', or safe channel mentioned by Leland in the mid 16th century. The 'cutting open' of the haven in 1676, blamed for the problems which ensued, presumably took place at the Old Stade, and as Mr Hewlett suggests in his 19th century report, the cause of the trouble was the diversion of the freshwater stream from the east towards the west. The water, now flowing into the sea at a new place, served to move and undermine the shingle at the stade with disastrous consequences for the houses built there and the capstans on the shore. If the author's opinion for the location of the sluice of 1654 is correct, then the new stade near the hoy may have been at the end of Stade Street, hence the name of that familiar Hythe thoroughfare. On the 1842 Map of Tithes, Stade Street is shown as 'The Stade' for the whole of its length.

At the beginning of this account, reference was made to newspaper articles by Mr George Wilks, a former Town Clerk of Hythe. Article number ten includes quotations from a survey of 1680, which was evidently made with a view to recording lawful landing places on the shore, between Jewess Gut in the County of Kent to Dungeness, and then to Eastware Point within a mile of Folkestone and thence to the stade at Hythe, the last named being 'that open place or stade containing 300 feet on each side of the bank or way leading from the sea to the Town of Hythe.'

Two further incidents involving the topography of the foreshore in the 17th century are relevant to this story of Hythe harbour. The first of these deals with the appearance of a structure called Sir William's Wall in 1682.

The grant from Sir Basil Dixwell in 1628/1629 concerned a right of way across his slipe. Since the right of way led to the haven, there is some value in looking further at the location of this area described as the 'slipe.' By 1682, it was in the possession of Sir William Honywood who expressed his intention to build a wall to enclose his slipe and wished to join his new wall to

another already in existence and belonging to the Corporation of Hythe. The wall built by Sir William was, in essence, an elementary coastal defence, and the line of the wall is shown on the Tithe Maps for the parishes of Newington and Cheriton in the early part of the 19th century as running from Seabrook towards Fort Twiss. The Fort was just about where Beaconsfield Terrace now is, at the eastern end of Marine Parade. The site for the Fort was acquired in 1795 by the Principal Officers of the Ordnance.

Sir William's Wall was doubtless an earthen bank and, according to surviving documents, by December 1682 two hundred rods had been constructed with the rest expected to be completed by Candlemas next, i.e. by February 2nd 1682/83. The purpose being to stop ingress of the sea, there was also a need to allow fresh water to drain into the sea, and for that purpose a pinnock or drain was to be installed. *(Middle Map & Diagram I, p 11)*

The Corporation Assembly for the 8th January 1682 reported on the matter and the Minutes record that the join between the two walls would be at the eastern part of the New Innings Wall of the Corporation. The same Minute also indicates that the area of the slipe was 120 acres. Sir William wrote as follows, addressing his letter 'These to the Right Honble. Robinson Beane Esq. Mayor and to the Jurats and Commons and Counsell of Hythe: Evington the 3rd December 1682'

> *"Mr Mayor and Gentlemen,*
>
> *I suppose It cannot be unknowne to you that I am Inclosing my grounds called the Slipe Joyning to the Innings Lands two hundred Rods of wall for that purpose being allready made and the Rest att furthest by Candlemas next will be finished for that the prevention of any danger that may happen to the Innings by the Irruption of the sea as well as floods by the fresh I judge it may be convenient as well as for you as myself to Joyne my wall to yours and to lay a pinnock in some convenient place for the sewing of both. I desire suddenly to meet together and to consult upon the premises.*
>
> *That I may (have) your minds in writing hereupon and if there be any scruple in your concerning these matters I will upon any notice give you a meeting and discourse it friendly with you.*

*In the meantime I am,
Gentlemen,
Your humble servant,
Wm. Honywood."*

Taking the rod as 5 1/2 yards at the time of writing, the length of wall completed was 1100 yards; that distance, taken with the 120 acres, fits the area between Twiss Road and Seabrook reasonably well.

The Corporation, concerned for the preservation of the right of way granted by Sir Basil Dixwell in 1628/29, which according to documents of the time was 24 feet in width, arranged for a deputation to meet with Sir William and were prepared to agree to the joining of the walls provided the right of way was preserved.

A further inference to be drawn from the documents associated with this matter is that the proposed connecting wall crossed two channels of the Corporation, and also that by the time of the joining, the harbour was stopped up by a wall built by the Corporation. There was also concern on the Corporation's part that the crossing of the two channels would run the risk of fresh water flooding on the Hythe side, and that in turn suggests that the two channels were still relevant for drainage purposes.

Fort Sutherland is on the right of this view drawn by D.Cox. Fort Twiss just visible on the left. Tower no.11 is built, 12 & 13 are not suggesting a date of around 1804. The large area of water in the centre marks South Road and the smaller to the right may indicate the position of the West Channel.

The way to the sea from the town, named Stade Street, is still a familiar feature to residents of present day Hythe. The word 'stade' occurs in old documents, and it appears to mean a quay or landing place. Before leaving this survey of the topography of the foreshore in the 17th century, an attempt will be made to locate a place referred to in two leases dating from Christmas 1695, one to John Lee, a maltster, and the other to Thomas Chapman, a fisherman. Both speak of the 'old stade'.

The leases were of sand or gravel grounds to be used for the purpose of kettle net fishing. The lease to John Lee covered 'that part of the Corporation sands or gravel grounds reaching from the confines of the Liberty of the Town and Port of Hythe and part of a wall lately erected by Sir William Honywood to the east, to the furthermost mark post set up at the old Stade for a common landing place towards the west, containing in length by affirmation 320 Rodds of Assize, more or less, and in breadth from the low water mark to the high water mark all along the full of the beach there, being part of the Royalty of Fishing belonging to the Mayor, Jurats and Commonalty.'

Thomas Chapman's lease was similar, but concerned a length of the shore again of 320 Rodds of Assize, from the mark post set up at the old Stade for a common landing place to the east towards the Willop Reach and westward.

On the basis of 320 rods, at 16 1/2 feet to the rod, each lessee had a mile of foreshore for his usages. These leases, and similar ones to John Combes, a barber, and Richard Clarke, a glover, in the year 1702, imply that the 'old Stade' was one mile westward of Twiss Road, which would put it somewhere east of the Fisherman's Beach, at the end of St Leonard's Road, although one has to ponder the accuracy of measurement, whether by 'affirmation' or not. *(End Map)*

Another pointer to the position of the old stade, though far from convincing, is the existence of a water channel, marked on the 1842 Tithe Map, and also mentioned in the Assembly Minutes for 1772, which ran from where Arthur Road now is towards St Hilda's Road. In 1772 Henry Tritton was given permission to make bricks at the channel and paid 2d. per 1000 bricks made. If the channel, marked on the middle map as the Great or West Channel, was at one time open to the sea at the western end, there may well have been an entrance there to the harbour.

The second incident related to the foreshore occurred shortly after the advent of Sir William's Wall. In 1688 a dispute arose between a tenant of Sir William Honywood and a tenant of Thomas Tournay, himself a tenant of the Corporation. The land in dispute is shown on a rough sketch or plan, bearing neither scale nor date, preserved with archive papers which include witness affirments as to the past occupancy of the disputed piece of land. The area of disputed land, shown on middle map near the eastern entrance channel to the haven, is based upon the sketch plan mentioned.

John Terry, whom we have already encountered, affirmed that he had been tenant of the piece of land in question, having taken over a lease granted to Thomas Strood in 1672, John Terry's tenancy, according to his evidence, having ended about 1680. Now the words of John Terry's lease dated 1677, do not suggest that he had possession of the land between the southern end of the thoroughfare now called Stade Street and the eastern boundary of the Liberty; but the witness affirments suggest that he did. On that footing, in 1677, the description 'Outlands and Beach Lands' could include land between the Innings and the foreshore, the present day locations of South Road and Marine Parade.

Two deponents stated that the fence between the disputed piece of land and the land to the east no longer existed, and a third person, who stated he had known the land for 46 years, gave evidence that the bounds of the parish and the Liberty of the Town were always reputed to be in a straight line from the head of the Town's Wall to the sea. This is a fair indication that the boundaries of the parish of St. Leonard Hythe, and the Liberty of the Cinque Port of Hythe, were coincident. The reference to the bounds being in a straight line from the head of the Town's Wall to the sea suggests that the land in dispute lay close to the sea. As shown on Map 2, the Town's Wall would not have served much purpose had it not come close to the foreshore, and the effect of joining Sir William's Wall and the Town's Wall would have been greatly diminished if the join had been at any appreciable distance inland. This third witness also said that the Lord Warden's Royalty was always reputed to extend westward from the wall, whilst the Royalty of Sir Basil Dixwell's predecessors had extended eastward from the wall. About 13 years before, a Dutch ship had come ashore just westward of the wall and against the land in question, and the Lord Warden claimed the anchor and cable as being within the Liberty of the Port. From that evidence, the piece of disputed land lay just westward of the boundary of the Liberty.

Another witness stated that the Corporation received duty for vessels coming up the Channel to the north side of the disputed land, though there was no indication as to where the vessels had come from or where they were going. The same witness also gave evidence that the Corporation took soil from the piece of land for the purpose of strengthening their wall when there had been occasion to do so, and were 'want to bring it crosse the Channel in boats'.

John Terry said little in his evidence, except to affirm that his stock 'had always ranged over the peece of land in question, and noe person ever questioned him for it, and Thomas Strode was the Town's Tennant before this affirment and enjoyed the same privilege of his stocke going on the said peece of land.'

These witness affirmations in 1688 confirm other items of information which indicate that the Innings area needed the protection of walls built to check sea flooding the pastures. At some time after the joining of Sir William's Wall and the Corporation wall, the name of Sir William's Wall seems to have been attached to the whole length, including the Corporation wall to the southern side of the Innings, for that is the name marked on the Tithe Map of 1842 and other maps. The last traces of those old walls seem to have vanished, although one does occasionally talk with elderly Hythe residents who have recollections of the last remnants of the walls in the Recreation Ground area.

According to a lengthy entry in the Assembly Minutes of 1st February 1753, a committee of the Corporation had reviewed old documents from 1682 relating to the joining of Sir William's Wall to the Corporation south wall. There is also a note in these Minutes that in 1739, a previous committee had been formed to make a similar review and report to the Corporation, but a memorandum in 1741 reveals that no such report was made.

> *"Be it remembered that Sir William Honywood Bart. hath last summer (i.e. in 1739) laid a penstock thro' his wall near the Beach of the Towns Channell into his to the eastward at his own expense, which memorandum this Committee (i.e. the one appointed in 1741) are of the opinion and humbly submit it to the Determination of this House is very inaccurate for it plainly appears by the old Books and Entries that the wall meant here belongs to this Corporation and not to the late Sir William or the present Sir John Honywood and it further appears to this Committee that there is at present and time out of mind has been an old penstock in the four acres of the Corporation Land joining to the slipe which sews into Sir John Honywood's slipe."*

In this Minute, the 'Town's Channell' seems to include an eastward extension of the West or Great Channel running towards the Slipe, eastward of Twiss Road. *(End Map)*

The cause of this interest in earlier events arose because the tenant of Sir John Honywood's slipe in 1753, one Thomas Taylor, had fitted a stopcock to the penstock and was evidently thus interfering with the drainage from the Corporation side. The outcome was that the penstock was opened and the Corporation complaint satisfied.

A further point of interest arising from this entry in 1753 is that the grant of a right of way from Sir Basil Dixwell in 1629 was of a 'way of Twenty four foot in Breadth to and from the said slip with carriages from the sea way to the Haven.' The description of a 'sea way' to the haven is unusual.

The mention of 'Sir William's Wall' in the Assembly Minutes of 1753 is a reminder of the fact, previously mentioned, that the Corporation south wall was eventually included in the overall name 'Sir William's Wall.' Some decades later, in 1814 there is a record in the Minutes of a rearrangement of a piece of Corporation Innings land, then occupied by Stephen Quested. A plan showing the changes appears in the Minute Book, and it can be related to features to be seen at the time of writing. A small piece of land near the end of the New Walk, later to be called Lady's Walk and now called Ladies Walk, was taken into the piece occupied by Stephen Quested, and another small piece he already occupied was to be attached to Innings land tenanted by Henry and William Tritton. In the description of these small changes, the term 'Sir William's Wall' was applied to the whole length, and it seems that the wall was still important at that time to protect the Innings from flooding. *(see flooding diagram p11)*

The Flood of 1877, described by Denise Rayner in 'Flood, Fire, and Sudden Death in Old Hythe'.

> *" A Gale sprang up about 8 o'clock in the morning; the wind gradually veered round to the south-west and reached almost hurricane force. High tide was around noon. From Fort Sutherland on the Ranges to Sandgate there was little to stop the sea except for a few houses on Marine Parade. Stade Street was the main road from the sea, and the water poured down this as far as the High Street. All available boats were brought into service as the water level quickly rose in the houses south of the Canal. The occupants of the Hope Inn had to be rescued from their upstairs windows.*
>
> *The Ladies Walk Bridge, then a narrow wooden footbridge, was swept along to Stade Street. More serious was the loss of Scanlon's Bridge, better known as Hang Gallows Bridge, which was an important carriageway . . . The sea came over the Duke's Head Bridge as far as the Brewery on the north side of Market (now Red Lion) Square. Some High Street shops had up to three feet (nearly one metre) of water in their lower rooms, particularly the older ones, where customers went down a few steps into the shop"*

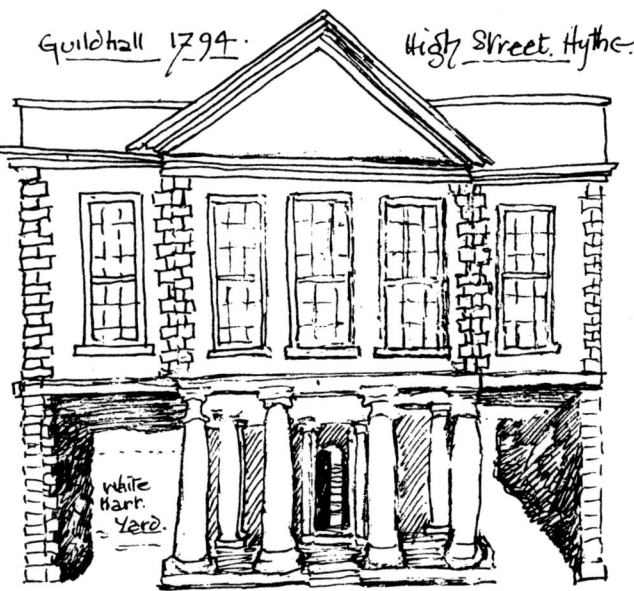

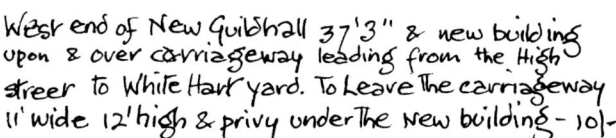

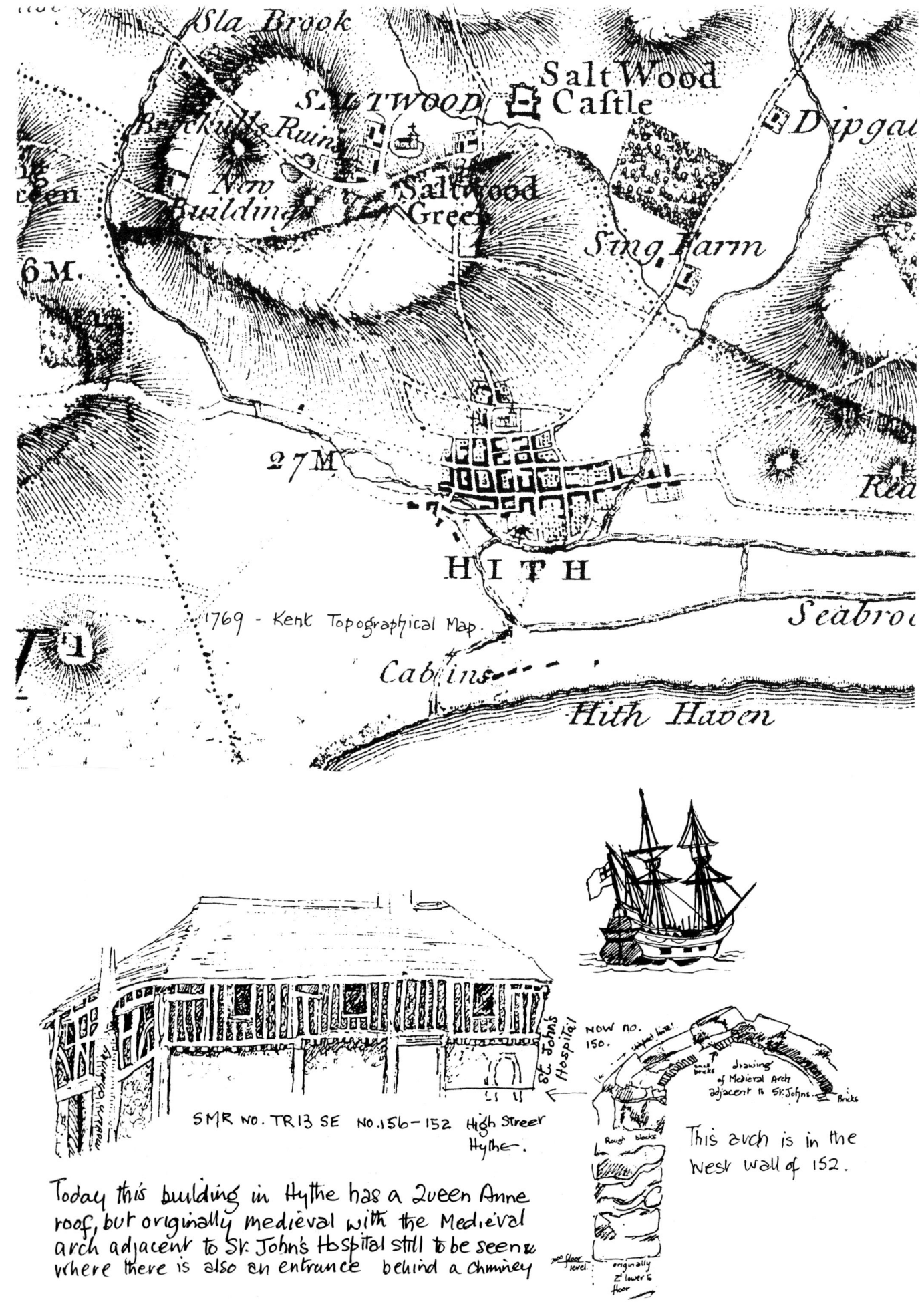

1769 - Kent Topographical Map.

SMR No. TR13 SE No. 156-152 High Street Hythe.

Today this building in Hythe has a Queen Anne roof, but originally medieval with the Medieval arch adjacent to St. John's Hospital still to be seen, where there is also an entrance behind a chimney

This arch is in the west wall of 152.

Chapter VII
Last Days

The writings of Mr George Wilks and Mr H. W. Hewlett have already appeared in this account. As a reminder, Mr Wilks was a former Town Clerk of Hythe, and Mr Hewlett was an adviser to the Crown. They were both involved in a dispute between the Council and the Crown over the ownership of the Hythe foreshore. A series of newspaper articles written by Mr Wilks and published by the Hythe and Sandgate Advertiser in 1884 and 1885, included quotations from a report by Mr Hewlett. As the newspaper articles followed a search of the Town Council records, they provide valuable illumination to the story of the harbour.

According to Mr Hewlett, by the term harbour or haven which occurs in the extracts from the Assembly Books, we can picture a lateral creek, which was probably the outflow of two or more freshwater streams. The outlet to the sea had become choked by the fifteenth century, and despite attempts to clear the channel, had again become choked before the middle of the seventeenth century. Judging from the previously mentioned Shorncliffe decree of 1679, this ancient channel or outflow ran towards the east, and entered the sea at the place now called Seabrook. Thus, for some distance, the channel, once the way to the haven, ran more or less parallel to the shore. Mr Hewlett supposed that the stade was situated on a ridge or full of shingle which separated the silted channel from the sea. There may have been a stade there Mr Hewlett visualized, for in the 8th year of Queen Elizabeth the First, a survey reported a haven within the Liberty and a stade without the Liberty. That may have been the 'old stade' referred to in various documents. The present author's opinion is that the 'old stade' lay further west.

Among the documents associated with the dispute between the Council and the Board of Trade over the ownership of the foreshore is a bound report by Mr Wilks entitled 'Hythe Foreshore', and some of the paragraphs may usefully be quoted.

"The sluice referred to in Mr Hewlett's report must have gone down to the low water mark, or otherwise the outlet would have been choked although the penstock or sluice valve would no doubt be beyond the reach of the tide, probably on the full itself or on the landward side of it.

Then again, the cutting out of the haven or harbour, looking to the rise of the land, no communication could have been made with the sea unless the foreshore was cut through, and the entrances which were choked up must have been between high and low water mark; the entrance could not have been above high water mark.

There was an entrance to the haven from the sea at a place near the present Number 13 tower. This was the last entrance, and was the one referred to which caused so much trouble and expense to the Corporation to keep open. No doubt the gates and sluices were, as supposed by Mr Hewlett, above or at high water mark, on top of the full, but there must have been works outside down to low water mark, and it was upon these works that all the money was expended to keep open the haven. There is no doubt as to this, the piles, planks and rock work have been taken up from time to time by persons now alive, and at certain times some of the old works are still to be seen.

When the haven became finally closed about two centuries ago, a new stade or landing place was erected - this was no doubt above the high water mark - but upon the closing up of the haven it became necessary to provide for the exit of the fresh water streams, and a new sluice was built at the place called Twiss Fort. The penstock and gates of this sluice were at the landward side of the full of the beach, but the sluice itself went down nearly to the low water mark; it was made of timber and was in existence within the present century, within the recollection of many now alive."

It is interesting to note that these paragraphs, written in the 1880's, contain references to old structures still in existence at that time which have now vanished. Some features remain. Martello Tower Number 13, is a private dwelling at the time of writing. It still stands near the western end of West Parade. The fact that there were once signs of some substantial structure there, or nearby, which was known or thought to have been connected with the harbour, is compatible with the source documents which tend to indicate there was an entrance to a channel in that vicinity a long time ago.

The reference to a 'sluice' by Fort Twiss seems to mean a drain or other outlet for the fresh water. The small sketch plan drawn on the Corporation copy of the lease for Fort Twiss shows a diverted channel and a 'new' and an 'old' bridge both crossing a channel marked close to the shore. Fort Twiss has long gone, although the name Twiss Road remains. During the course of coastal defence works in 1995, some blocks of stone which bore obvious signs of the mason's art were exposed on the foreshore opposite Beaconsfield Terrace on Marine Parade, near the seaward end of Twiss Road. These seem likely to have been part of the former fort rather than remnants of an old sea wall.

A decree of 2nd February 1726 may well be the best evidence of the location of the sluice constructed in 1654.

> 'Whereas of late years the Innings Lands have suffered much damage from fresh water floods, it is therefore ordered that the land owners of the said Innings Lands shall have liberty to lay a Gutt through the Sluce Hole wall, they making good the said Gutt in repaire by an equall Scott or rate to be laid on the said Innings Land and to be paid by the proprietors of the said land.'

If the sluice of 1654 was constructed in the Common channel, then the words of this decree make sense, for the Innings lay to the eastward of the position of that channel. But not if we regard the sluice as being at the western end of the West or Great Channel.

The fragmentary information upon which this account is based has been used in an attempt to describe the fate of the harbour of Hythe in the late 16th and 17th centuries. It appears that the harbour in 1591 was on an east to west channel, located more or less parallel to the shore, and fed by freshwater streams running in a common channel leading from a confluence near the town. An 'old stade' seems to have been situated near Fisherman's Beach, and a new one created in 1679 at the end of Stade Street. Despite constant efforts over the years, the tidal channels became choked, and in an effort to overcome the problem, in the middle of the 17th century, a sluice was apparently built across the common channel for the purpose of impounding a head of water for flushing out the channel. As this sluice would have blocked the common channel near the seaward end, navigation towards the town would have become impossible after the construction of the sluice. Traces of the old harbour may well have been obliterated by the construction of the Royal Military Canal in the early 19th century, when the engineers would have avoided excavation work by using existing old channels wherever possible.

The time has come to leave the vanished harbour of Hythe in peace. Whatever the doubts and uncertainties left to linger by the available facts, one thing is certain; that the play of the wind and the sea, which combined to bring about the demise of the harbour and caused so much change in centuries past, is set to continue. That much is history in the making.

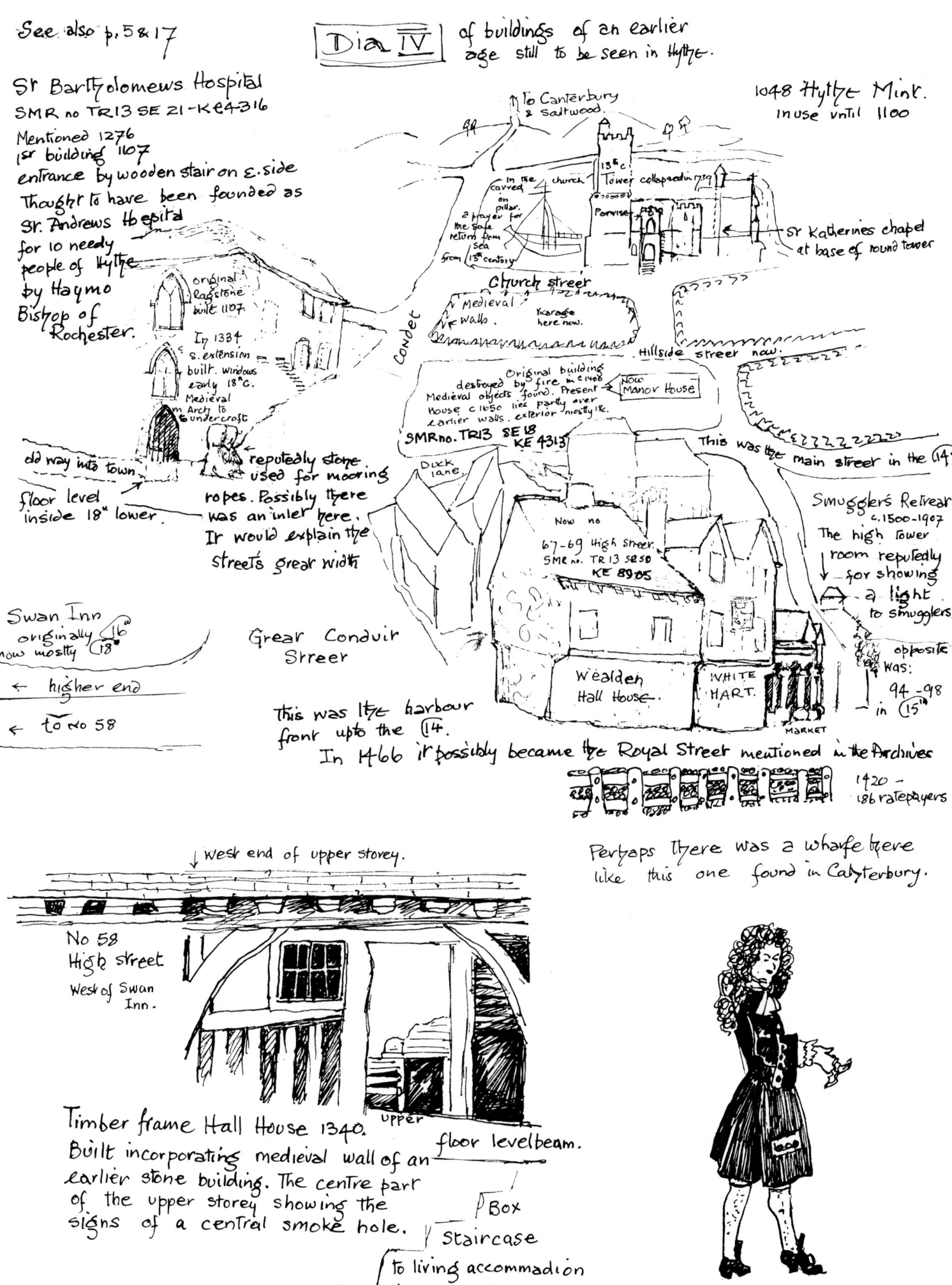

Sources, Bibliography, Acknowledgements

Hythe Town Archive

Minutes of Assembly of the Corporation of Hythe:- 1580 to 1591, 1608 to 1624, 1624 to 1635, 1635 to 1641, 1649 to 1683, 1683 to 1783.

Transcription and translation of Jurats Book of Accounts 1412-1413, Revd. T.S. Frampton 1885, archive item 1053.

Att. Gen. v Mayor, Aldermen and Burgesses of Hythe; papers concerned with a dispute over the ownership of foreshore at Hythe, 1883 to 1889, archive item 1292.

Counterpart copies of leases granted by the Corporation of Hythe and similar documents:-

Lease of lands to Edward Cressye 1570-71   HyT4/3
Lease to Martin Allynson, 10.3.1574   HyT2/2/1
Lease to the sons of Daniel Langdon, 1st January 1603   HyT2/6
Lease to John Terry, 20th March 1667   HyT4/12
Lease to John Lambert, 20th July 1677   HyT/16
Lease to John Lambert, 10th May 1686   HyT4/21
Lease of sands or gravel grounds to John Lee (1695, HyT4/23) and
    Thomas Chapman (1695, HyT4/22)
Lease of kettle net grounds to John Combes and Richard Clarke, 1702   HyT/26
Lease of pasture land to Thomas Tourney, 30th April 1685   HyT/20
Lease of pasture land to the Principal Officers of the King's Ordnance, 2nd February 1795
Transcription and translation of the Charter of Queen Elizabeth 1st. 1575

'Letter about cutting out the Harbour'   archive item 1132

Papers concerning a dispute between a tenant of Thomas Tourney and a tenant of Sir William Honywood, 1682   archive item 1284.

Folkestone Local Studies Centre and Library

Map of Tithes for the parish of St. Leonard Hythe 1842
The Municipal Records of Hythe, 1884-1885   G.S.Wilks   942.23
The Barons of the Cinque Ports, 1892   G.S.Wilks
New English Dictionary
Dictionary of National Biography
The History of Dover Harbour   Alec Hasenson, 1980
History and Topographical Survey of the County of Kent   Hasted, 2nd Edition, 1798
Collection for a History of Sandwich   William Boys, 1792
English Social History   G.M. Trevelyan
Life in Norman England   (Batsford)
Life in Tudor England   (Batsford)
Life in Elizabethan England   (Batsford)